# Franchising

# Success Basics

*A Guide For Future*

*Franchisees*

JE Johnson, MBA

**Cataloguing in Publication Data**

JE Johnson

Franchising 101

Description: Crimson Hill Books trade paperback edition | Nova Scotia, Canada

| | |
|---|---|
| **ISBN:** | 978-1-989595-52-7 (Paperback - Ingram) |
| **BISAC:** | BUS105000 Business & Economics: Franchises<br>BUS048000 Business & Economics: New Business Enterprises<br>BUS060000 Business & Economics: Small Business |
| **THEMA:** | KJVF -- Franchises<br>KJB -- Business studies: General<br>KJH – Entrepreneurship |

Record available at https://www.bac-lac.gc.ca/eng/Pages/home.aspx

Front Cover Image: Picjumbo, Pixabay.com

Book Design & Formatting: Jesse Johnson


Crimson Hill Books
(a division of)
Crimson Hill Products Inc.
Wolfville, Nova Scotia
Canada

Crimson Hill
Books

# Is a franchise business in your future?

Wish you could go into business for yourself, not by yourself?

If so, investing in a franchise could be your golden opportunity.

Franchisees enjoy a higher rate of success, compared to solo start-ups. They also reach profitability faster.

One reason for this is when you buy a franchise, you don't have to re-invent the wheel, because the business model and strategy are already proven. So are sourcing, pricing and marketing, among other risk-reducing advantages franchisees enjoy.

Yet, like any major purchase, you need to go in eyes wide open.

Even with franchising, success is not a guarantee. And it's not for everyone.

Could it be ideal for you?

This book gives you the information you need to reach well-considered answers. Here's exactly what you need to know before you commit!

1. **Do you long to be in business for yourself, but not by yourself?**

2. **Are you concerned about the high risk of business ownership? The high number of businesses that fail before they are even a year old?**

3. **Do you seek a real opportunity where you determine how much you can earn, with no 'upper limit' to your earning power or your success?**

4. **Do you dream of creating a new and better life for yourself and your family, but you don't want to start a business from scratch?**

5. **Do you have some money to invest? Do you want to put your money to work for your future?**

If you can sincerely answer **YES** to these questions, then a franchising could be exactly what you're looking for!

But what type of franchised business could be right for you? And how does it work?

What do you get for your investment of time and effort? And what could you expect in return?

Read on for the information you need now to make an informed decision about franchising and if it's the best path forward for you ...

Think of a friend (or perhaps a family member or a former colleague) who has made it in his or her own business.

Picture what he or she is doing right now.

Sure, they're working. They're probably working just as hard as anyone with a 9 to 5 job. Maybe harder. Possibly for longer hours.

But do you ever hear him or her griping about the boss, the hours, the endless commute, or the fact that they haven't gotten a raise (or a promotion) for ages?

Not likely.

What you do hear is how their working life is a challenge, but they love it. They're busy, maybe even too busy sometimes. But they're not just plodding along, like most people do, living paycheck to paycheck and secretly wondering if life is just passing them by.

**They've realized the dream of working to achieve a better, happier, healthier life. They're doing what they love, running a successful business.**

And they're thriving. Their enthusiasm shows. They tell all their friends about how great this new life is. So that's got you wondering, "Could this same magic work for *me*?"

Think about it. Could you fire the boss, invest in your

own business and make the leap to self-employment?

Could *you* be one of those people that get written about in success stories in the business pages of newspapers and in trade and national business magazines?

The short answer is yes, it can happen. Success as a business owner is a do-able dream. This book will reveal the basics about the best and fastest way to achieve that dream. It is **franchising**, a way of doing business that gives you everything you need with a proven success system. Becoming a franchisee provides the training and support to help you achieve that success in the fastest (and most trouble-free) way possible.

If you go into your new franchised business venture eyes wide open, thoroughly informed and you have made a careful choice that truly reflects who you are and what you want next in life, you, too, could become one of the thousands of people who succeed in business through franchising.

Chances are you already have what it takes to succeed:

1. **Life experience**, including having developed good people skills as an employee and perhaps a manager
2. **A strong desire to succeed** by following a proven formula
3. **Savings** to invest, plus a solid credit rating
4. **Excitement** about taking on a new challenge

5. **Passion** for your product or service and for serving customers

6. **Energy and ambition** combined with **a 'can-do' attitude**

Here's what you ***don't*** need:

**1.** *A university degree in accounting or marketing –* though it's certainly helpful if you do happen to have this background, it isn't necessary.

**2.** *A truckload of cash.* You'll need financial fuel to power this dream (like almost every venture in life), but it may be less, possibly much less, than you imagine. For most franchise opportunities, the total financial requirement is in the $50,000 to $350,000 range, with $150,000 being average.

For some opportunities, the costs of admission are higher, but many are far less (as little as $3,000 or so if you are looking for a part-time or home-based opportunity). Only about half of this money needs to be in ready cash – with good credit, you can borrow the rest.

If you are ex-military, a woman, or a member of some other groups such as racial minorities, there may be government grants or loans available to help launch your business. Find these with an online search, or you may hear about these programs at Franchise Shows.

**3.** *A track record as a skilled worker in/or manager of the same business (or similar) as you are now thinking of investing in.* One of the great strengths of franchising is that, by design, it allows you to transfer skills you already have to jumpstart a new business career. Franchisors have already invented and developed all the systems you'll need.

**4.** *The 'right' connections or membership in the 'old boys' business community* – franchising is equal opportunity, accessible to all.

If you want to be in business, and you want the fastest, easiest, least-risky way to become a business owner, franchising may be your answer.

This book covers the basics with everything you need to know as you begin your search for the *ideal* franchise opportunity and the key to unlocking your happy and rewarding future! At the end of the book you'll find a Glossary describing the most common terms you will hear used by franchisors and franchisees.

## Franchising, franchise, franchisor and franchisee – are these all just words for the same thing? Or is there a difference?

**Franchising** is a method of doing business in which the owner grants the right to conduct one or more outlets (called **units**) of that business for a stated period of time to an individual investor (or group of investors) in exchange for a fee plus royalties.

A **franchise** is the brand name of the business, such as one of the major burger or pizza chains. Sometimes "franchise" refers to one outlet of the business.

The **franchisor** (or **franchiser**) is the company that owns or manages the franchise. Franchisor can also refer to the founder of the company and the management team at head office.

The name of the brand and the franchisor are usually, but not always, the same. One common submarine sandwich franchise, for example, is both a fast food franchise and a franchisor, but the British company that owns a well known chain of ice cream stores is the franchisor while the actual franchise operates under the name of the ice cream stores.

A **franchisee** is a person who wants to be in business but avoid most of the risk of an independent business start-up and so has invested in a franchise rather than go into business on his own or her own. A franchisee may invest in just one or several outlets of one, or more, franchises. A multi-unit franchisee owns more than one outlet (or unit).

## I have read that you buy a business, but you invest in a franchise. What's the difference?

When you purchase a business, you (and your lenders) own it, along with all its possessions (or assets) and also any liabilities (outstanding debts), just as you would after purchasing any other big-ticket item such as a house or car. Just like any other major purchase, the business remains under your ownership until you sell it or otherwise legally dispose of it.

Franchising is different than ownership. Think of it as being more like leasing a car or renting a home. You get to enjoy the privileges of ownership, under certain conditions, for, usually, a well-defined period of time. At some point your stake is 'used up' because you have enjoyed all, or nearly all, of the benefits. In franchising, this time period is called the **term**, and the contract between the franchisor (the company) and the franchisee (you) is the **Franchise Agreement**.

What is left at the end of a term, if it is not going to be renewed, are the tangible assets the franchisor owns (the location), the tangible assets you own (stock, possibly office supplies) and the intangible assets, known as the **goodwill** you have built up in the business. Tangible assets and Goodwill are usually saleable assets.

Franchise Agreements can have as brief a term as five years, but most are for 10 or 20 years, and then are renewable under conditions stated in the original agreement, usually in increments of five years up to a total of an additional 20 years beyond the original agreement.

## What is the Franchise Fee, when is it paid, and what do I get for my money?

The Franchise Fee is the fee payable to the Franchisor when you sign a Franchise Agreement.

It can be any amount set by the Franchisor, from as

low as a few hundred dollars (rarely) up to several hundred thousand dollars (and, for some franchises such as hotel banners it can go into the millions of dollars.

The Franchise Fee may vary by the unit size you plan to open, for example whether it is a full-sized operation or a mall kiosk or, in the case of a service franchise whether you plan to begin the business working part-time rather than full-time.

Some franchisors also have a 'sliding scale' of franchise fees, depending on how many potential customers you will have in your territory. Urban territories are likely to be far more lucrative than small town or rural and the franchise fees reflect this.

While it may appear that Franchisors are making their livings selling franchises, (and this may be the case with the few dishonorable franchisors) in general franchisors don't earn their money by selling franchise agreements (but they may have Franchise Brokers who do).

For most Franchisors, it actually costs more than the amount of the franchise fee to find and qualify prospects and then get new franchisees trained and their businesses up and running.

Because the success of the franchisor is completely dependant on the success of the franchisees they choose as partners, franchisors tend to take great care in the selection process, which can last several weeks to several months. For the most capital-intensive franchised ventures, such as restaurants and hotels, it is not uncommon for a year, or longer, to pass between signing the Franchise Agreement and the first day in business.

Here is what you receive from the franchisor in exchange for the money you pay up-front for the franchise fee:

- The **right to use the brand and the franchisor's knowledge assets** such as copyrights, trademarks, leases, trade secrets (an example is a secret recipe), or purchasing agreements for the term of the Franchise Agreement;

- The **Operating System** (also known as the OS), which is presented during training and spelled out in detail in the Manual (this is the how-to 'Bible' for running the business);

- The initial **training**, usually two to six weeks at Head Office or, for the largest systems such as Subway, at one of their regional training centers. Note that training costs are included in the franchise fee, but your travel costs to get to the training location, plus accommodation, meals and most other expenses while there are usually *not* included in the Franchise Fee;

- Access to **on-going training and support from the franchisor**.

In quality franchise systems, training is ongoing throughout the term of the agreement. Some of the types of support offered are:

1. Help in selecting and obtaining your location. The franchisor usually owns the location for larger franchisors such as QSR (fast food) restaurants and usually doesn't for the smaller

franchisors.

**2.** Store design

**3.** National and regional marketing and assistance with local/regional marketing

**4.** On-going training

**5.** Assistance with obtaining your opening inventory

**6.** Assistance obtaining leases on necessary equipment, machinery, or vehicles

**7.** Preferential supplier contracts

**8.** Customized accounting or staffing software.

Some franchisors also offer help obtaining financing and a few offer their own finance programs to highly qualified franchisees.

There will also be a stated number of 'visits' from someone at head office to see how you are getting along. These are usually twice a year, possibly supplemented by more frequent visits from a master franchisor (see Glossary at the end of this book for definitions) if there is one, or an Area Representative of the franchisor, two or three times a year or as needed.

There may also be **Annual Conventions** offering opportunities to learn about new products and services, other company initiatives such as marketing, regional seminars and meetings, a franchisee newsletter, a franchisee council giving franchisees the opportunity to offer their input to the franchisor, and other supports such as training or productivity incentives for franchisees' employees;

A **network of colleagues** who are the other franchisees in the system available (by phone, e-mail and online conference calls and perhaps in person) to offer help.

You will get a list of the system's franchisees as part of the disclosure documents you receive before signing the franchise agreement and can ask for a complete list, if you haven't already received it, on signing the agreement.

In most systems, you get **assistance with location selection**, and in some the location is actually 'assigned' to you or you are taking on an existing location because the current franchisee is retiring or leaving the business.

## What is a deposit agreement?

Before letting you in on any of their trade secrets including their financial statements, franchisors may want some concrete indication that you are a serious prospect, not just someone who may be trying to learn whatever you can before joining their competition. To help protect their interests, these franchisors ask for a deposit, such as $5,000.

This deposit is regulated in some states or provinces, so see your lawyer (be sure to choose a lawyer who specializes in franchising law) before signing anything.

If you are a serious contender and, in order to proceed to the next stage, you are required by the franchisor to pay a deposit fee (given that it is legal where you plan to do business), deposit money should be placed in trust with your lawyer or the franchisor's lawyer rather than with the franchisor or it's representative.

If you decide not to continue with the application process, conditions for full or partial return of your deposit must be stated in the deposit agreement.

## Who are most franchisees? What type of person succeeds in franchising? Is there an ideal franchise personality? Or set of skills?

Generally, people who succeed in franchising are people who succeed in life. That is, people who are practical, optimistic, enjoy working with people and take responsibility for their own success. They know how to work and they know how to motivate people around them.

That is where the list of traits they have in common ends.

There are successful franchisees of every adult age, race, gender, from many backgrounds with a range of skill sets and working life preferences. Franchising offers a variety of opportunities.

If you are willing to investigate the broad field of

franchise opportunities and choose carefully, eyes wide open, and then work to make your franchise choice a success, you, too, could find yourself joining the ranks of successful franchisee-franchisor partnerships.

## What are franchisors really looking for when they screen potential franchisees?

Franchisors are looking for new franchisee partners who are positive, upbeat and excited about the opportunity and the brand because, as any good salesperson will tell you, if you don't like the product, your customers aren't going to, either.

Passion counts. In fact, it can tip the scales in your favor when you don't quite reflect the profile in other ways (such as, for example, being younger or older than their 'average' successful franchisee).

They want to know that you are 'their kind of people'. This means you fit the profile of their most successful franchisees. The most successful franchisees are people who are sales-oriented, high energy, with persistence and drive, plenty of self-confidence, a genuine interest in people and a willingness to follow the established formula.

They look for outgoing people who truly enjoy serving customers, even the 'difficult' ones, who are optimistic, practical and adult. Like any employer, they also look for a strong work ethic.

They want to know that you have enough money, both to get going and to stay in business long enough to succeed (without putting yourself or your family in dire circumstances). There are a lot of variables, but typically, a successful new business will achieve profitability somewhere between the one to three year anniversary of opening.

Commitment, honesty, integrity, maturity, responsibility – all the things good parents teach and you would value as a customer are also traits held in high esteem by franchisors. They want to know that you are going to join them in making customers' needs and desires a priority.

Family values are important. It may sound hokey, but franchise businesses tend to align with conservative suburban middle-class family values. While the fast food outlets have made no secret that working class/middle class families are their prime target, the fact is that the majority of customers of almost all franchisors' businesses (not just the 50 per cent or so that are food banners) are working people in family mode who buy franchise products and services to help them ease, or enhance, family life.

Holding a business degree or having a background in business management isn't a requirement, though if you do have this background you have an advantage. Most franchisors say if you have common sense, ambition, some sales and business experience and realistic goals, they can teach you their specific business in two weeks or so of training. If you are a reasonably intelligent and committed person, you can pick up the rest on the job.

You don't have to have been a restaurant manager or a chef before you become the owner of a restaurant, but it helps to have some familiarity with either the food or hospitality business OR some business background so that you will have realistic expectations. If you haven't, it is a good idea to try it on for size – even if it is only for a week or so as a volunteer staffer. Then ask yourself if you'd be happy spending the next 10 or 20 years of your life in a similar environment?

If you have little business background, you may want to skill up in this area. Libraries and bookstores are well stocked with books on business basics. Or you may choose to enroll in a basic course at your local college.

What have you accomplished in life so far? A franchisor will have legitimate concerns about someone who doesn't have a solid work record, some recognized accomplishments since leaving school or who seems to have moved around too much, or who doesn't appear to be active in their community.

## Is there any type of person who does NOT succeed in franchising?

Yes. You may have some or even most of the characteristics franchisors seek, but if any of the following also describes you, franchising may not be such a good choice:

- **Strong need to be the leader** or to be the boss. Franchisors seek team players with strong collaborative people skills.

- **Need to be entrepreneurial**, to invent the business and make decisions about how it will be run. Although franchisors often say they are looking for "entrepreneurs" or people with "entrepreneurial spirit," in fact what they seek are people comfortable with following a system that has already been established and proven its ability to generate success. Franchisors are looking for good lieutenants, not good generals.

- **Desire to be a 'passive investor'** or absentee owner. Franchising is a hands-on opportunity.

- **Desire for plenty of variety or independence**. The OS is a proven system. The franchisor invents it; the franchisee follows it. Mavericks need not apply.

- **High level of creativity**. While there is some scope for creative and personal expression, especially with young, small or new banners, in general in franchising there is less scope for creativity than you would have in an independent business.

- **High degree of patience**. Franchisors have found that people who are 'laid-back' and very easygoing are less likely to succeed in franchising than are more assertive go-getters.

- **High degree of impatience**; low tolerance for frustration. As with any business, there is a learning curve, and success does not come overnight. Or, as many franchisors are fond of saying, franchising is a 'get rich slow' opportunity.

- **Desire to be semi-retired,** or work a 'short' day or and 'easy' week or to work different hours than the usual hours of operation for this type of business. The average franchisee works a 60-hour week, including their business open hours plus doing such tasks as payroll after-hours. However, if you do want to exchange your high-stress big city life for the slower pace of a small town, franchising does offer such flexible options as partnerships, or (in some service systems) working part-time.

- **Preference to work alone, uninterrupted**. Occasionally this may be true, perhaps when doing the books in a home office. However, most of a franchisee's time is spent with people, including staff and customers.

## What are the reasons a franchise application would be rejected?

- *Financial* – you do not have the assets (savings, a home to re-mortgage to free up funds or use to secure a loan) and you do not have the borrowing power (a strong credit rating, friends or family members willing to lend money).

- *Personal* – the franchisor has reason to doubt your motives (are you merely buying a job?) or questions how serious you are about working fulltime (and possibly overtime in the early years) to build your business.

- *Professional* – you have owned a successful business in the past (and therefore may prefer to be independent; may be unwilling to follow the Franchisor's Operating System, the OS) or you have owned the same business in the past. Some fast food franchisors, for example, automatically reject former restaurant owners as franchisees because they don't believe the new franchisee will be willing to follow *their* system.

- **Skills** – Some basic business sense plus 'people' skills. Specifically, can you sell? If you don't like sales, franchising is probably not for you.

- **Fit** – this one is elusive, but it comes down to, "Is the franchisee our kind of person?"

## There seem to be a lot of franchises out there. Which one should I invest in?

True, there are a lot of franchisors to choose from. It is also estimated that franchised businesses account for half the total annual retail sales. Here, as in every developed country in the world, franchised businesses are thriving. Their numbers are growing. Projections are that trend will continue through this century.

The good news is that this vigorous growth means there is at least one franchise out there that is *ideal* for you. The downside is that it may take you some time and research to find it amidst the huge number of options.

First, you need to separate the quality franchisors from the fly-by-nights and get-rich-quick schemes. Generally, if a franchisor is a member of a national franchising association, it has agreed to comply with a defined level of ethics in business dealings far above any legislated either federally or in your state.

There are quality franchisors that are not members of these International Franchise Association affiliates, but one of your questions to them might be, "Why not?"

## Finding the right franchise seems overwhelming. Where do I start?

The answer to this question begins with some careful thought about who *you* are and what *you* want in life.

Think of the jobs you have had in the past, and what you liked best (and cared least for) about each. Make lists. Do you see patterns emerging?

Next, consider your successes in life to date, including successes in your work, leisure and other non-career activities.

What do these experiences have in common? What did you achieve? What did you learn? What was most satisfying about these experiences?

Who were you working with?

What type(s) of people do you most prefer to spend your working life with?

Consider when you want to work -- time of day, mornings, usual office hours, just when the kids are in school, evenings, weekends, summers only?

Where do you want to work – primarily at a desk in

your home office, or in clients' homes, at clients' businesses or at a store counter? Maybe mostly outside?

Where do you want to live – your current city or town or...? Do you want to live in another part of the country?

How much variety do you need? How much routine? How much travel (or perhaps you want no travel required?)

Once you have answers, think about them. Ask family and friends, the people who know you best and care about you, for their insights. What do they think you would be successful and happy doing (and, just as revealing, why?). What do they recommend you avoid?

Consider both what works for you and what will suit your family if relocating will be involved.

***Think about your ideal workday***. Let your mind take you there. Imagine what you do, from the moment you wake up. Where to you go to do this work? What sort of work is it? Who else is there, and what is their role?

Take another careful look at the dreams of your youth and young adulthood that you may have abandoned in order to get an education, climb the career ladder, or take care of other goals and commitments.

That dream of living in a friendly small town on the coast, or opening your own health food store in an exciting city you've always wanted to live in, or doing what? Where? Paint the picture in your mind and then paint yourself into that picture. Does it give you joy just to think about it?

Allow yourself to image you are there, in the situation, living that dream of success in business and in life. You are starting your working day, arriving at your own place of business. How does it feel?

It's easy to get the idea that most franchise opportunities are fast food outlets, because they are so visible in almost every city (and town) not to mention in advertising messages. In fact, QSR (Quick Service Restaurant) accounts for only about 40% all franchisors, meaning there are plenty of other choices. Look around and you'll be astonished at the sheer variety of types of businesses that are franchised.

Here are just some of the types of businesses listed in directories I checked (in of late 2020) that are franchisors with territories to offer new franchisees:

# SERVICES

- Accounting or Tax Advice and Preparation
- Advertising, Marketing or Public Relations
- Automotive
- Building and Design
- Business Equipment Rental
- Business Consultants
- Office Space Rentals
- Tutoring

- Child Care
- Cleaning
- Home Repair, Renovation
- Custom Deck Building
- Transportation
- Lawn Services and Landscaping
- Environmental Services
- Clothing Rental
- Financial or Investing Advice
- Fire Safety and Home Alarm Systems
- Fitness, Health and Nutrition
- Furniture Repair
- Smart Phone Repair
- Hair and Nail Salons
- Spas
- Home Inspection
- Home Staging
- Hotels
- Campgrounds
- Home or Office Painting
- Real Estate sales, Property Management
- Weight Loss centers
- Travel services
- Sports and Recreation
- Home Care for Seniors

# PRODUCTS

The products list is shorter, though there are more opportunities than listed here; this is just a sampler:

- Advertising and Promotional Products
- Automotive or Truck Parts and Rentals
- Cosmetics or Beauty Supplies
- Environmental Products
- Pet Supplies
- Many types of Retail Stores – Dollar Stores, Family Discount Department Stores, Mobility Equipment Sales, Clothing Stores and those specializing in baked goods, candy, baking supplies and more.

For further inspiration, look on the franchise association websites already listed, or buy one of the annual franchise directories available at bookstores or at your local library. (See Resources at the end of this book).

## What is the actual process for becoming a franchisee, and how long does it take?

It varies, depending on the size of the franchisor, their recruiting strategy and availability of locations in areas you're interested in.

Usually, your approach will start with a phone call, perhaps in response to an ad you have seen, or a listing in a franchise directory. Some franchisors will provide basic information about their opportunity during this initial call; but most will want to find out more about you (pre-qualify you as a prospect) before they send an information package, a franchise application, or both.

Before providing information, most franchisors will ask you to fill out a pre-application report. It asks about who you are, including current and previous work experience, annual salary, education, family situation, hobbies, community involvement and a financial profile with credit references. They will also ask for personal references, if a spouse or family member will be involved in the business, whether you have ever been self-employed and why you are interested in their banner.

The franchisor will also want specifics about your financial readiness to proceed. They will also be looking for signs that you have thought this through and understand the commitment you are making to them and, potentially, the promises (covenants) they will be making in partnering with you.

If the franchisor sees potential based on your answers, you will receive a Franchise Information Kit. This kit, despite the name, is a sales tool with the sole purpose of generating qualified applications.

The sales kit usually contains:

- a company history,
- testimonials from successful franchisees,
- a (glowing) list of benefits should you choose to join them in this business,

- projections of income and expense,
- a summary of the initial investment required,
- reprints of articles about the company, and
- recent ads and other marketing materials.

While it does have some information, the info kit is primarily a sales tool. The main purpose is to get you to send in the completed application.

Next, if they like what they see in the application, you will meet with a representative of the franchisor, at their office or your home. This is their opportunity to learn more about you, and your opportunity to ask questions.

At this point, they may ask you to sign a confidentiality agreement, stating that you will not reveal what you are about to learn about the company. The sales rep may also want you to complete a personality profile (this assigns a number score to such traits as degree of extroversion, patience, conformity and need for dominance).

Generally, there will be a second meeting with the franchisor's representative to focus on the financial opportunity. At this point, the franchisor will provide a copy of their Disclosure Document (this is required by law to be given to you a stated number of days, at a minimum, before you sign the Franchise Agreement). If it is legal to do so at this point in your state or province, the franchisor may also ask for a deposit and require an Interim Offer to Purchase. All of these documents should be reviewed by your attorney before you sign anything.

Next, you receive the Franchise Agreement, have the

opportunity to discuss it with the franchisor's representative, and usually have the opportunity to meet managers or (in smaller franchisors) the president or CEO. Location will also be discussed.

Finally, the Franchise Agreement is signed, the location arranged, you are booked for the next training session, and you receive the Manual. You pay the balance of the franchise fee, go to the training, take delivery of your equipment and inventory, complete other site improvements and prepare for the big day – your Grand Opening.

## What is a Disclosure Document?

Documents supplied by the franchisor to prospective franchisees containing information intended to help the prospect make a fully informed decision are known as Disclosure Documents. They contain information about the company, its managers, history, current and former franchisees and financial health. In some states and provinces, the specific information the Disclosure Documents must contain and when they must be delivered to a prospective franchisee are mandated by law.

If you do not live in one of these places that requires detailed disclosure, but the franchisor operates in a state that does, it will have detailed disclosure documents prepared and you (or your lawyer) should ask for them, if they are not offered. Study them carefully and ask all of your questions (your lawyer and accountant are your best resources to help with this) before signing.

## How likely am I to be accepted, once I fill out an application?

On average, franchisors accept about a third of the people who complete the application process. The odds improve in your favor if the franchise is smaller (fewer than 40 units) or newer (less than ten years in franchise format) or a success abroad but new to the country or your region or if you already are an employee of the franchise or one of its franchisees.

Odds of being accepted are lower for the larger, more established banners, and for the largest ones, you may have only a faint hope of being selected. The mega-banners always have a waiting list of qualified franchisees, making them the toughest to get into.

## An article I read says I need to do my "due diligence" before investing. What does this mean?

Due Diligence is a business term meaning all of the investigation a company would need to do when buying a major asset (such as a division of another company) before completing the purchase agreement.

In franchising, due diligence also refers to all of the careful research and investigation you need to do before you invest in a specific franchisor's system as a new franchisee. This includes finding out everything you can about the franchise and making sure you understand all of the information you collect.

This book is just the start of your due diligence. Here are more sources of good information:

To learn more about the many franchisors there are, read small business and franchising magazines and directories. You'll find them at bookstores, your local library and at the libraries of colleges and universities with business programs.

Attend a small business or franchise trade show. These are held annually in most major cities. Much like a car show or a boat show, the banners are on display, with sales representatives of the franchisor at the booths talking up their opportunities.

Franchisees of the franchisor you are interested in are a good source of information. Call them up (the franchisor will provide a list of their current and former franchisees to serious prospects) and ask them what they like, and what they don't like, about dealing with this franchisor.

Does this franchisor honor agreements? Are franchisees pleased with the products or services, the suppliers and what they are charged for supplies?

If they had it to do over, would they make the same choice? Why, or why not? If you hear a few gripes, chalk it up to human nature. More than a few could be a warning sign. Rarely, you will read about mutinous franchisees in the business pages. Do an online search to find out what franchisees are saying. Their gripes could be legitimate, and something you'll want to avoid in your future business.

Franchise consultants and lawyers or attorneys who specialize in franchising are another source of information. Ask franchisees for referrals.

Try to talk to customers of the franchise that you are interested in to find out what they like, and what keeps them coming back.

Go to at least three outlets of the banner, possibly in another area (perhaps while on vacation) and pretend you are a mystery shopper – how good is the service? How happy are the other customers? Is it your kind of place? Can you imagine yourself working here and enjoying it? Can you see yourself getting up each morning, eager to work with staff and customers of this business?

## There is a franchise trade show in a city near where I live coming up soon. Should I go?

Just as franchisors vary in quality, so do the franchise and small business shows. At the best ones, you will find you get a lot for the price of admission, including:

Free seminars on basics such as how to finance your new business and how to hire, train and keep good staff.

The opportunity to size up dozens (or, at the largest shows, hundreds) of franchisors actively seeking franchisees.

Information packages are usually available at the shows.

Shows can be noisy and crowded, with Friday evenings and Saturday afternoons being the worst times to visit. The best times to go are during a weekday, either mid-morning or mid-afternoon. If the weekend is your only option, try to get to the show right after opening (usually 10 a.m.) and go with your prospective partner (if there will be one) and, if you are married or soon will be, go with your husband or wife. By bringing your spouse, franchisors get the message that your spouse supports this venture. If your children are young and could potentially distract you during conversations with franchisors, it will be best to leave them at home.

Dress at franchise trade shows is business casual. Remember, just as you are sizing them up, they are also creating an initial impression of you.

Use the show as a meet-and-greet to gather basic information, get a name and contact number for those banners that interest you and expand, or narrow down, your options.

Here are some of the questions you might want to ask franchisor's representatives at trade shows:

- What is your target market?
- What are your plans for my area (or area you want to move to)?
- What are the franchisee's obligations?
- How profitable is a franchise in your system?

- What was your sales growth last year? Over the last three years?
- Is your franchise best operated singly, or as a partnership?

## Should I buy a big-name franchise or a smaller, less known one?

Both have their benefits.

With the big name, you can expect a larger franchise fee and more requirements, including higher capital needed, a more formal recruiting process, a longer time between signing and actually opening your business, and more structure. The benefit of the Bigs is instant brand recognition, and (usually) a faster time to profitability.

Building up the business will definitely take longer if you sign on with a banner that is small (small is defined as less than 40 units) or relatively new (has been franchising for five years or less) or both established and successful elsewhere, but new to your part of the world. In this case, you can expect a lower franchise fee, possibly lower capital requirements, but also more opportunity to help define the brand rather than merely toe the line that's already well established.

The first option is 'safer' for the risk averse; the second offers a bit more scope (but not a lot) for creativity. Either has led to success for many franchisees and potentially can for you, too.

# Should I buy into a franchise that is successful elsewhere in the world or in another part of the country, but new in my area?

Yes, if you like being a leader with a new product or service, if you have done thorough due diligence and are convinced that the concept will 'translate' to your community, and if you are able to be patient about how soon you achieve profitability.

Here are some things to ask yourself when considering a franchise import:

- Where will the support come from? Will I have a master franchisor, or area representatives to call on when I need help? Or will I need to rely on managers at a distant head office?

- What local and already established competition is there for this product? Why do I think people here will find the newcomers' products or services superior to what is already available?

- Are there cultural issues that might make it popular in its area (or country) of origin, but possibly not here?

- Are there translations needed for product packaging, customer instructions, signage, etc.? If so, who will pay these extra costs?

- Does the foreign franchisor expect franchisees here to help it understand the American or Canadian market? Or other things that may be different, such as standard business laws and practices here?

- Pricing – can the product or service be priced competitively for this area, while still allowing me to make a profit?

- Supply sourcing – Will I be required to buy (import) product or its components (ingredients) or materials from a distance (or abroad) and what costs will that add? How long will it take? Or can I source locally or regionally?

- If the franchisor is foreign, what about currency exchange issues?

Also if the franchisor is offshore, you will need the services of a franchise lawyer experienced in international franchising.

## Where do I find a lawyer experienced in franchising laws?

Ask for recommendations from your state or provincial law society. You can also look at the member directories of franchise associations (see Resources at the end of this book). Franchise lawyers and consultants are usually members of these associations. Their directories are online.

## Are there any types of franchises to avoid?

Trust your common sense.

Think carefully about the business, and ask yourself if it is a product or service people want, need, and are willing to pay for not only today, but for the coming decade or two (or is it just a fad or trend?).

Beware of franchisors that use heavy pressure tactics to get your money before you have had a chance to do your due diligence, or who are in businesses where there is already significant, and strong, competition with little differentiation between products (that is, you would be hard-pressed to create a competitive advantage in your market with the product or service).

A well-known franchise consultant advises his clients to choose a franchise system that appeals to a cross-section of the market, not just a narrow band of that market, avoid franchises that are targeted to customers of a particular ethnic group and avoid saturated markets.

## What is a corporate store?

A corporate store is a store owned, and usually operated, by the franchisor. It may be that it is the 'first introduction' location for new products or a new décor or new 'style' of outlet the company plans to introduce across the system. It may be the site of training for new franchisees. It could be the flagship store in the system, or one that the franchisor has taken back from a former franchisee and is running until a new franchisee takes over.

You want to choose a system that has a thriving corporate store, because this demonstrates that the Operating System (OS) does work. But be aware that the financial structure is different for corporate stores (for example, they do not pay royalties and usually will have lower expenses than the franchised units) and so their financials may not reflect the same results you can expect as a franchisee.

## I know that I need legal help before I sign and my brother-in-law, who is a real-estate lawyer, has offered to do it.

Good for you for looking for ways to save money, but this could turn out to be a false economy. In the long run, you will be better off investing in the services of a lawyer who specializes in small business and specifically in franchising.

Here's why:

You get an expert who knows the franchisors and, if necessary, can steer you clear of shady operators.

A franchise lawyer will also have a strong working knowledge of the current and pending legislation, both federal and state or provincial.

Through their own industry network, they can help you make valuable connections and put you in touch with other experts or help you get additional information.

Because they are 'in the loop,' they will have heard of

both good opportunities and ones to avoid.

Most critically, they can walk you through documents such as the Franchise Agreement, Offer to Purchase and your lease, explaining every aspect fully and answering all your questions – or helping to see that you get the information you need.

## Should I also have an accountant?

Yes, because they can help you understand the financial information provided by the franchisor and evaluate how realistic the company's projections of earnings and ROI will be in the case of your own future business.

An accountant who specializes in small business can also help you make a realistic assessment of your financial risk and how much debt you can comfortably manage. Tax is another area where an accountant can help.

To find an accountant, ask franchisees in your area, or contact your local CPA or CA association for referrals.

## What can a franchise broker or franchise consultant do for me? Why do I need one? How do I find a good one?

First, recognize that there is a difference between a Franchise Broker and a Franchise Consultant.

The Broker is a sales person, working on behalf of a franchisor (or several franchisors) to find, qualify and recruit new franchisees. In some places, their business methods are regulated; in others they are not.

A Franchise Consultant usually works for clients who are franchisors, helping them improve their businesses in a number of ways such as brand development and possibly including their franchisee recruitment methods and policies.

However, there are some Franchise Consultants who work directly with franchisees and prospective franchisees. Among their services are assistance in finding the right fit between franchisee and franchisor, sales of existing franchises (when a franchisee wants to exit the business or retire before the end of the term of his or her franchise agreement) or assistance in getting financing.

**I have read some real horror stories about people who had a franchise and when it failed they lost their life savings. How can I protect myself?**

You are wise to be wary and to take a hardheaded, careful look before you leap. About five percent of franchisees fail each year. The good news is that this failure rate is less than half the failure rate of independent businesses.

Reasons for franchisee failure are similar to the reasons for franchisor failure:

- **Poor fit**. Making an impulsive choice; failing to fully investigate before signing the franchise agreement/offer to purchase; unrealistic expectations.

- **Poor financial management** or **poor planning**, including not enough capital to get through lean times, catastrophes (such as a fire or flood that closes the business during repairs) or threats such as a strong new competitor.

- Failing to anticipate lower-than-expected sales due, for example, to a rise in interest rates or a downturn in the economy that causes widespread unemployment.

- **Straying from the Operating System (OS).**

- **Failing to keep premises clean and attractive.**

- **Failing to pay attention to product and service quality.**

- **Not hiring and training efficient, competent staff** and/or failing to retain good workers; poor staff morale, high staff turnover.

- **Neglecting the business.**

- **Poor location choice** (not enough traffic; rent too high).

- **Failing to make friends in the community**.

Recognize that although franchising is a way of reducing business risk, risk can never be eliminated. The best ways to protect yourself are:

- **Hire good experts** – specialists in small business with a track record specifically in franchising. Ask plenty of questions. Don't sign anything until you understand it fully.

- **Do your homework**. Don't rely entirely on your team of experts to spoon-feed all you need to know. Talk to people in business, especially franchisees in the business you intend to start. Observe the business and similar businesses (including the competition)! Form your own assessment of how strong this company is, how focused on growth, and how able it is to achieve its goals.

- **Think** carefully. Is this really the right opportunity for you?

- **Forecast**. Prepare for both the best-case and worst-case scenarios (most businesses get some of both) for your own unit.

- Don't allow yourself to fall in love with the banner until you have taken a long, careful, critical look at the numbers. **Choose with your head *and* your heart**; but head first.

- Then, **plunge in**. Don't fall victim to analysis paralysis. Expect glitches, some frustrations, and even buyer remorse (very common after any major or life-changing decision, and this is both) while you make this transition to your new life. Most franchisees have some wobbles at the start; most who persevere do just fine.

## How can I recognize a franchisor that's in trouble?

There are many ways, falling into two broad categories – your impressions (or gut feeling) when you meet the franchisor or franchisees or visit their locations and the story their numbers have to tell.

Be wary if:

1. You feel you are getting the hard sell rather than being invited to form a new business partnership.

2. You hear a lot of griping from franchisees, especially if it is about poor products, poor support from head office or lack of communication.

3. Customers aren't happy (or there aren't enough of them).

4. The franchisor insists that any lease incentives offered by developers or landlords are payable to the franchisor rather than to franchisees.

5. The franchisor doesn't want you talking to current or former franchisees.

6. The franchisor insists on prepayment of royalties – as much as three years in advance.

7. The franchisor avoids answering your questions.

### *Do franchisors ever fail, and if so, why?*

Yes they do.

Reasons include:

- The Franchisor may have weak (inept, distracted, or simply under-motivated) management.

- It may have failed to respond to or anticipate market demands and consumer trends or the strength of its competitors.

- It may have run into cash flow difficulties (generally because of under- performing franchisees).

- It may have lost key supply contracts and failed to replace them.

- It may have 'drifted' from its concept, thereby alienating its core customers.

- It may have tried, unsuccessfully, to reposition itself in the market.

- It may be 'stale' with outdated design, décor, products, packaging, image, etc.

- It may have grown too quickly, bringing on more franchisees than it was prepared to support efficiently. Or it may have grown too slowly, thus not generating the revenues the franchisor needed to develop and market the brand.

## What happens if the franchisor declares bankruptcy?

This worst case scenario is something you will want to discuss with your lawyer **before** you sign. It could be that you are able to add a provision in your franchise agreement specifying the outcome you would like in the event that your franchisor steers into troubled waters. One possible option you lawyer could suggest is an exit clause.

Generally, as a franchisee you may only be minimally affected if your franchisor develops financial difficulties, for example as they operate under creditor protection as they attempt to get their finances in order; ultimately succeed, and move on.

Or, as a franchisee you may take a larger role, such as finding that you need to reassure your customers that, although the banner has encountered difficulties, it is business as usual for you and the other franchisees. In this situation, you and the other franchisees may want to organize a Franchise Committee that deals specifically with the bankruptcy and various possible outcomes.

Among these possibilities are:

- The franchisor changes ownership or 'cleans house' and acquires a new slate of managers while slashing its losses (such as non-performing franchise units) and, possibly with a décor update and refreshed products, goes on to success. A number of franchisors have accomplished this in recent decades.

- A franchisee group could buy the company, in effect becoming the new franchisor, and continue successfully.

- The franchisor fails, but many of the franchisees continue in business as independents, perhaps with a name change but the same products and suppliers.

## What are my options if the franchisor changes ownership?

Franchise companies can be acquired by even larger, perhaps multinational, companies. Or they can become public (meaning the owners are shareholders of the company's stocks, traded on a stock exchange) or, as one major franchisor recently did, go from being publicly-traded to a privately-held (in this case, family-owned and directed) company.

These changes may not affect the franchisees, or they may have a profound effect. For this reason, discuss this with your lawyer. A new owner may bring in new resources. On the other hand, they may increase franchise fees or be inexperienced in this business and, as a result, make some serious mistakes, such as allowing product quality to decline or abandoning the core business.

You may want to have a clause written into the Franchise Agreement that if the banner changes hands, you have the option to exit.

## What is the best franchise to buy?

You will see plenty of 'best of' lists in business magazines and on websites but remember that there are a lot of ways to define "best."

Best large, best small, best to start in a small town, best for someone who'd rather spend most of his time out-of-doors and hates having to work at a desk, best for someone juggling work with parenting young children...there are so many ways to describe "best."

This is also true when looking at "best" and financial

return: best gross sales, best net, best ROI, best margins, fastest sales growth, best inventory turnover are all indicators of performance. If you don't already know these terms, and what is the most appropriate 'best' in the type of business you plan to start, ask your accountant to explain these terms and help you analyze you franchise choices.

In terms of best overall for both the money and the lifestyle, only you can answer this question: what is best for you? Once you have, there are many ways to learn if the franchisor you plan to partner with is an ethical business and if their claims regarding franchisee expectations of success are legitimate or pure blue sky. Are they a member of a national franchisor association requiring adherence to a high level of ethics in all business dealings? (Such organizations were also the first to require that all member franchisors provide disclosure information that still, in almost all jurisdictions, exceeds what is required by law).

Be thorough in you due diligence. Talk to current franchisees. Make it a point to talk to former franchisees of the systems that interest you. Check out the franchisors' web sites. Have a look at the many online forums where the discussion is about small business and business start-ups.

## I recently spotted an interesting franchise concept while on vacation abroad. Could it work where I live?

Maybe.

One of the interesting things to observe in other countries is the businesses that appear to be successful, sometimes hugely successful, but are unknown back home. While some of these franchisors are happy to remain in their country of origin, others are open, and perhaps actively looking for, North American partners.

It could be your golden opportunity. But beware – there are always additional costs involved when you 'import' a concept successful elsewhere, but new to your area. In the case of franchises from Europe, for example, one big cost will likely be translation of all of the business documents and marketing materials.

Unless you are already fluent in the language of the franchisor's home country, communication with head office could be another hurdle, as will dealing with a franchisor successful in a different culture and time zone.

 Becoming the franchisee of a foreign franchisor is more complex, and likely to be more costly (import duties and delays, for example, and the cost of currency fluctuations). And the banner adored by the French or a hit in Britain may leave North American consumers cold.

Engage a franchise lawyer with international experience to help you fully assess the opportunity.

## What franchises make the most money the fastest?

Franchising is not like winning the lottery or inheriting a fortune. Actually, it is more like most things in life – you get back what you put into it. You make your own luck.

The beauty of franchising is it provides almost anyone with an opportunity to start a business that has a higher than average chance of success. But, like all businesses, a franchise business is a combination of effort, potential and risk.

The benefit of franchising over independent businesses is to rev up the potential while reducing the risk (the effort remains roughly the same).

Franchisors tend to claim a 90 per cent success rate for all franchised businesses (including their own) while pointing to the very high failure rate of independent businesses (80 per cent fail within the first five years). You may want to ask the franchisor's representative for actual numbers for their system backing the success claims they make for the banner.

One major study analyzed the performance of over 18,000 American and Canadian companies, based upon data on their sales tax returns. They divided the companies into five business sectors.

The findings: franchised companies' performance ranged from 34 % to 314 % better than owner-managed independent businesses when measured by gross sales.

The differences depended on business sector, the experts concluded, with restaurants/fast food being the clear leader. This much better performance of franchises, when compared to independents, was due to gross sales as a function of the strengths of franchising: brand-name recognition and superiority in training, marketing, location and buying power, the experts concluded.

## How do the finances usually work? How much will the bank lend me to get started?

You begin by assessing your financial needs, both start-up and operating costs, also called working capital, including inventory and payroll.

You will need funds for growth (hiring new employees, additional inventory, new equipment) and to carry you through any lean times (for example, if a direct competitor opens across the street and launches a price war or interest rates suddenly rise).

There are two ways to finance a business, and it is likely you will use both:

- **Debt financing** is borrowing money from lenders such as the bank (called creditors) who will require repayment with interest.

- **Equity financing** is assets from owners, including your own savings and possibly money borrowed from family members or friends. In exchange for the money they lend, your equity lenders become shareholders.

While most franchisors cap debt financing at 50

percent, you need the advice of an accountant to determine how much debt you can comfortably manage. Too little, and your business may be cash starved. Too much, and debt load may doom your business from the start.

Keep in mind that banks will not lend you the money for the Franchise Fee. While a bank may be your first choice as lender, they are only one of several sources of financing. Beyond borrowing from family and friends, your other financing options include:

- Other conventional lenders such as trust companies, credit unions, insurance companies and finance companies
- Various small business start-up programs run by the government (though it is getting harder to borrow from them)
- Private (angel) investors
- Supplier loans
- Leasing rather than purchasing assets
- Grants or loans designed to bring specific types of people into business ownership, for example women, members of minorities or ex-military.

There are other ways to finance a franchise. To learn more, ask your accountant.

It is typical for new franchisees to borrow a third to half the amount needed.

Some franchisors also have programs in place helping qualified managers or staff of their current franchisees with a 'work-to-own' arrangement that results in a much lower cost up-front to get their business going.

Franchise consultants and Franchise lawyers can steer you to franchisors currently offering these types of opportunities.

## What franchises can I get into for less than $50,000 in cash?

There are some, but increasingly it is becoming a short list.

Though there are some franchises that require less than $50,000 for the Franchise Fee, which is most of your cost to get started (unless you will need to build your location and you will own the building and the land under it) but remember that you will also need money to operate the business until it is profitable and you will need money to live on in the meantime.

Operating expense (working capital) is the amount franchisors state under "capital required" in their franchise directory listings, and the reason why the average investment is $250,000, of which only part is the Franchise Fee.

## Are there any franchises that I can get into for less than $20,000? Less than $10,000? Less than that?

While the average total investment is about $250,000, with about half of that in debt financing, there are some franchise businesses you can start for less than that, and a few that cost far less.

Typically, the least expensive franchise opportunities are service businesses you would run from a home office and perhaps part-time. These opportunities may not be enough to provide a living income for you or your family.

If you seek a low-cost start-up, investigate the small and new or relatively young franchise systems because they offer lower franchise fees. In addition to getting started for less, as an early-entrant franchisee, you can expect to have fewer rules to follow and more say in the OS, perhaps helping to define the brand and the market in its early days.

Here are some examples of franchises you could start with an initial investment of less than $50,000, though the franchisor will also want you to have back up money (savings or borrowing power) to operate until you're in profit.

- Pest Control
- Landscaping
- Home Inspection
- Math and other types of Tutoring for Children
- Maid Service, Janitorial Services
- Homecare for seniors
- Shuttle services
- Furniture Repair
- Movers

One downside of investing in a banner that is small or

new is the same as the benefit; fewer rules. But you'll also be called upon to help build the brand and introduce it to customers, rather than have a waiting market anxious to have a local outlet for products and services they already know, like, trust and are eager to become loyal to. It may also be a system that hasn't yet fully proven itself. For this reason, your risk with a newer franchisor is higher than with an established banner.

With the pool of qualified potential franchisees being much smaller than the number most franchisors would like to be able to choose from, some have concluded that there could be candidates who are exceptional in every way, but lack the necessary capital and they have developed programs to help good candidates find the money.

Other franchisors are specifically targeting groups who are still under-represented among the ranks of franchisees, specifically members of minorities, veterans and women.

Some franchisors have become truly creative in helping franchisees (qualified in every other way) get financing. One uses an in-house finance program that lends up to 80 per cent of start-up costs, with the other 20 per cent coming from the franchisee's own assets. The application process is quick, interest rates and terms are designed to be competitive (with conventional lenders) and loan decisions are made within two or three days. Franchisees have up to seven years to re-pay.

Another franchisor does more than simply help franchisees with their loan applications to conventional lenders. It also finances up to half the franchise fee, store design costs and equipment package.

Another creative program for attracting ambitious new franchisees is a large North American convenience stores work-to-own program, available to corporate store managers who make the grade. That's how one franchisee, who started out as a sales clerk and was promoted to manager, got her big break, investing just $3,500 from her savings to open her store in 1998. The company financed the franchise fee and inventory cost, which totaled $ 93,500. Her gamble and hard work, with a leap from employee to franchisee, has paid off. By 2000, gross sales at her unit had grown 30 percent to a healthy $1.5 million.

Franchisors who once limited their franchisees to the larger urban centers in the belief that any place with a smaller population could not possibly support the business have taken a second look at that assumption and are now adding units in smaller cities and towns. To do this, they have developed a 'smaller' model of their concept which is less expensive to open that their traditional units. One example is a family restaurant with seating for 70 rather than their traditional 130-seat unit.

Another way franchisors are opening units in cities or towns they once dismissed as "too small" for growth is by *co-branding*. Co-branding is sharing resources, such as a location or staff, when one, or both, are franchised businesses.

That is what the owner of a successful wrecking

business in a suburb of major USA city did when he wanted to expand his business. Looking for an opportunity, he discovered there was a need for a rental car agency. None existed nearby, and people in his part of town had to drive a distance just to rent a car. After doing his due diligence, he invested $5,000 for what the director of franchise sales for a car rental franchise specializing in low cost rental calls their "least expensive" option, a protected territory of up to 9,999 people.

The franchisee started with just three rental cars. Within two months he had increased his fleet to 12, and soon opened a second location. He says his business "has grown from just something to supplement business to an entire business of its own!"

There are also franchisors that are actively teaming up qualified franchisees (who provide the sweat equity) with angel investors.

Your local Chamber of Commerce as well as your accountant or lawyer may also have information about franchisors that are creating programs with city and regional government and redevelopment agencies to open stores in underserved rural and urban areas.

## What is the actual total cost going to be?

There are so many variables, including your costs of borrowing and how much tax you will need to pay, that no two franchisees, even in the same system, will have identical costs.

It will not be possible to crystal-ball the precise amount of money you will need. But with care and the help of your team of experts, it is possible to come up with a pretty good estimate of what your financial needs and expected performance will be.

You will need to do these projections if you are approaching lenders. Even if you are not, it is a worthwhile exercise because it could help you avoid what could be an expensive and life-wrenching mistake.

Most franchisors offer templates and other help in preparing your financing proposal, as do the major lenders.

Since it serves no one to have an undercapitalized franchisee flounder and then fail, franchisors will want proof that you have enough money (your own assets and borrowing power) not only to start the business but also to stay in business.

Franchisors refer to *initial costs*, *initial cash required* or *initial investment* and exactly what they mean by these terms varies. It will be spelt out in the Franchise Agreement.

Total costs include:

- The ***initial franchise fee***, which must come from your own assets. Lenders will not provide financing for the franchise fee because it is considered an intangible asset.

- The ***advertising fee*** for opening advertising and promotion; critical to build traffic quickly. As a new franchisee you may be required to spend a specific amount on grand-opening advertising and promotion.

- **Site selection fee**. Some franchisors charge a fee in addition to the franchise fee for site selection and lease negotiation.

- Cost of **construction or leasehold improvements**. These costs can be reduced through tenant incentives, which are discounts, offered by landlords to new tenants.

- **Purchased equipment** and **costs of storage** (if necessary) pre-opening. Lenders usually require that you purchase new equipment; though buying used can save you money. Franchisors often use their buying power to purchase equipment and most franchisors pass these savings along to their franchisees.

- **Inventory** is usually purchased by a new franchisee.

- **Pre-paid expenses** such as deposits on the lease, equipment leases, phone, Internet, and services including utilities and insurance.

- **Pre-opening operating expenses** (such as initial staff training)

- **Land** and the **building** (if not leased); mall fees (if a mall location)

- **Professional fees**: attorney or lawyer; accountant, franchise consultant

- **Miscellaneous expenses** – employee costs, banking costs, business license or permit, etc.

- **Working capital** including wages for your staff and yourself, rent, supplies and inventory.

These expenses can be handled through an operating line of credit.

## What are royalties?

Payment made by the franchisee to the franchisor for the right to continue in the business. This is similar to paying rent on the brand.

For this payment, franchisees receive ongoing assistance, training and support, purchasing power, product development and marketing research. The royalty fee is usually paid monthly and is usually a given percentage of the gross sales (all the money going in the till, less sales tax). Typically, the royalty fee is between 2% and 6%.

In some systems, rather than a percentage of sales, the royalty is a set amount or a fee based on the size of the franchisee's market, such as so much per 10,000 population in your trading area (protected territory).

Another variation, called *product franchising*, is when franchisees are required by contract to buy all product (or product components) from the franchisor. The franchisor earns its profits on the product while the franchisees in product franchising usually do not pay royalties.

## What is the Advertising Fee (also called Advertising Fund Contribution or

# Marketing fee)?

The advertising fee is your share, as a franchisee, of the cost of advertising materials and national or regional advertising in print (newspapers or magazines), broadcast (radio or TV) and online. It may also provide for co-op advertising, in which the franchisor matches, dollar for dollar, the amount the franchisee spends in regional or local advertising.

The advertising fee may be a set amount but more commonly is between 1% to 2% of gross sales (excluding sales taxes collected), payable monthly with the royalty.

How the advertising fee fund is spent (the advertising buying decisions) may be made at head office, or jointly between head office and a marketing committee made up of franchisees and corporate managers.

The advertising fee does not provide for all the advertising a franchisee will need to do. You will also have to budget for local PR and advertising to generate business for your own unit. Usually, franchisors provide guidance in how to do this.

# What is a transfer fee?

The transfer fee is the amount payable to the franchisor if the franchisee wants to sell the business back to the franchisor (who then has the task of finding the new franchisee for that unit) before the franchise agreement term has ended. Generally, there is no fee if the franchisee exits the business at the end of a Franchise Agreement term. There is a fee to renew the Franchise Agreement, usually stated in the original agreement.

## Are there 'hidden' costs of franchising? If so, what are they?

By the time you sign the franchise agreement, you should have a clear idea of what your expenses will be, including franchise fee, your lease (or cost to build), leasehold improvements (or cost of build-out), cost of opening inventory and normal operating expense (fixed costs and variable costs).

You will also be paying your travel and accommodation expenses for training, fees charged by your experts (lawyer, accountant) and for business services, such as insurance and local advertising.

## What is re-franchising?

This is the term some franchisors use to refer to their units (a store location or a territory) that had a franchisee in the recent past, but are now being run as corporate stores because the former franchisee has retired or exited the business for other reasons such as poor health.

The franchisor now seeks a new franchisee for that unit. Investment level for a re-franchise will be similar to amounts required of a new franchisee with a new location, although it can be higher to account for goodwill accrued in a successful unit. The big benefits to you as a franchisee in taking on a re-franchise are that it will be a turnkey operation and that it already has a customer base.

# Why do there seem to be so few women in franchising?

Until recently, franchising was dominated by men, primarily Caucasian males in their 30s or 40s among franchisees, and people who are similar but a decade or two older among franchisors.

While men are still in the majority in franchising, the face of franchising is changing as women and members of minorities, more young adults in their 20s and adults at mid-life (and beyond) are succeeding as franchisees.

Of all groups, women make up the largest group who are under-represented as franchisors and franchisees. When this trend was noted at one franchisor, "We thought we should get the word out to women that franchising is a great way to have your own business," said the president of this major fast food chain. This franchisor is among the franchisors that have launched successful programs in recent years with the goal of finding more female franchisees.

Today, one in five of this franchisor's franchisees is a woman. The president agrees that financing remains a major hurdle for many otherwise well-qualified franchisees, and that financing remains more difficult for potential franchisees who are women, in part because women, as a group, tend to be less willing to take a major financial risk.

Her company, she says, is among the franchisors that have responded by helping potential franchisees connect with angel investors "who've already created their wealth and want to diversify for a small piece of the action." In effect, they have created a mentoring program for franchisees.

## As a recent immigrant, I am required to start a business, which I also want to do to provide work for myself and my family members. Is franchising a good option?

Yes, it can be an excellent choice. Franchising offers a number of benefits for newcomers to this country including:

- The ability to get your new business up and running quickly.
- The proven success formula (the OS).
- Brand recognition.
- The ability to provide good jobs for yourself and family members

The support you will get from quality franchisors

includes a lot of handholding through the start-up process. This will be particularly important in starting a business in a culture (and possibly also in a language) that is new to you.

## I am a member of a visible minority and have heard that franchisors don't really want people like me. Will I face discrimination if I apply?

Unfortunately, there was discrimination in the past, and there have been well-publicized lawsuits as a result, as recently as the late '90s. While there is no question that old-boy and elitist attitudes still exist in Corporate North America, the most progressive companies have recognized how damaging discrimination can be and have taken positive steps to change.

Many franchisors are among the ranks of the enlightened. They have realized that the talent pool of franchisees is much smaller than their need for good people, and so they must broaden the net, not only because that is the law, but in order to have any chance to grow. And also, being good pragmatic businesspeople, they recognize that in order to be able to appeal to customers who are women or members of minorities, they need to be more inclusive, both in who they partner with as franchisees and suppliers, and who they hire as staff.

Some franchisors have taken this a step further, with

programs specifically designed to recruit more 'non-traditional' franchisees and give them various types of incentives, including help with financing.

## I have taken early retirement but find I'm not quite ready for the life of leisure. Is franchising a good option for me?

If you have plenty of energy, overall good health, and the challenge excites you, go for it!

You may want to look beyond the QSR and retail franchises to find the banners that offer the most flexibility in terms of work hours. If you prefer to work part-time, there are some franchisors that offer this option. Or consider teaming up with a partner so you each run the business 'half' time.

## I know this is what I want to do, but I'm only 23. Will I be turned down because of being too young?

No, youth is not a cause of automatic rejection, but it may be harder for you to arrange financing, and as a result more difficult to impress the franchisor's recruiter.

Your best bet will be to work for the franchisor or on staff at a franchisee's unit. If you like them and they like you, and you go in with enthusiasm, high energy and a killer business plan, you'll have a huge advantage over any other franchisee candidate, of any age.

# I have been offered a choice of buying an existing location that is a corporate store or another location directly from a franchisee who is retiring. What's the difference?

Corporate stores may be:

- Successful ventures that have had managers but never a franchisee
- Locations a succession of unfortunate franchisees have failed with
- May have been successful with a former franchisee that has had to exit the business suddenly due to, for example, major illness or in a more orderly fashion, as in when a franchisee retires before the end of the franchise agreement term.

You cannot assess the specifics of these two opportunities or compare them until you have all the facts. What has happened with both these outlets, and why? You and your lawyer and accountant need to take a close, careful look before making a decision.

# I have heard that there are several documents I will need to sign. What are

# they?

Aside from those required by your lawyer and accountant (dealing with bank accounts, tax payments, and employee deductions if you will have employees) there are a number of documents you will sign with the franchisor. These are:

- Franchise application (and possibly also a Franchise Deposit)
- Non-disclosure/confidentiality agreement
- Offer to purchase
- Lease documentation
- Franchise Agreement

## In the Franchise Agreement, what is negotiable? What isn't?

Lawyers claim almost everything in any contract is negotiable, while franchisors will tell you that nothing in their franchise agreement or other contracts with franchisees is negotiable. The truth, say franchise lawyers, is somewhere in the middle.

Franchisors believe that a 'one size fits all' franchise agreement is necessary for it to maintain control and provide consistency in its dealings with all franchisees.

That is true. But in practice no two franchisees have precisely the same situation and there is no such thing as a standard franchise agreement (that, some franchise sales reps may tell you, "everyone signs") and no two agreements will be precisely the same.

Sections regarding the following have points that are usually negotiable:

- Location
- Exclusive territory or 'protected' territory (always be sure this is fully defined in writing)
- Opening date
- Any points specific to a particular franchisee
- Exit clause – conditions defined

Generally, approved suppliers, products or services are not listed in the franchise agreement, but are in the operations manual, and these are never negotiable. Compliance with everything in the manual itself, along with all future updates to the manual, is enforced through the franchise agreement.

## What is meant by exclusive territory?

Franchises need to be close enough to each other to benefit from proximity such as, for example, being able to call your nearby colleague when you run out of a critical product or ingredient so you can borrow enough to tide you over until the next delivery.

But too close, and you will be competing directly with that colleague, and few things are worse than competing against your own brand. You want to have the franchisor's assurance that they have 'right-sized' the number of outlets under their banner in your area, that your area is yours (no customer poaching allowed; territories enforced by the franchisor) and that territories will not be re-drawn (they could shrink) in the future. Ask to see the evidence that the franchisor plays fair on the protected territory issue.

## What do I need to know about location?

There is a saying that every good corner in North America is already taken. While that's an exaggeration, the most desirable real estate for traffic and visibility in just about every city and town already has a fast food outlet in place. If you dream of joining the ranks of fast food franchisees, you can expect tough sledding in the location competition, unless you are taking over an existing unit (either a corporate store or from an exiting franchisee).

The same may be true of other types of commercial real estate in your city or town (or the one you plan to relocate to).

Consider the neighbour businesses. Here's an example: the neighbors are a dance studio that has the most traffic in the evenings. That won't work so well next to a movie theatre where all the parking may be taken most evenings.

A mall location will add operating expense, such as the requirement that a percentage of your gross sales is needed for the mall fee, or you must be open (and pay staff) during times when your customers do not want to do business. Consider how the location you choose may either add to, or cut into your profits.

For retail, location rules. Are there plenty of cars? Do traffic lights and near-by stores draw traffic? Is there enough convenient parking? If it is a plaza or mall location, is there a strong 'anchor' store near-by? Will the customers of the near-by stores logically become your customers?

Is visibility an important factor for your business? If so, where will your signage be? How visible is it from the street?

Business hours may be dictated by town or city bylaws or the mall or plaza landlord.

Keep in mind your customers' needs and what is most convenient for them.

Is the area growing, or in decline? Will your unit be close to where a large population either lives, or works, or both? How close are your direct competitors?

Location size is a factor in your success. Is there enough space for storage, maintenance, inventory, and supplies? But not too much space you won't need (but that will add expense)?

Lease terms – your lease should match the term of your franchise contract, but be renewable in shorter increments.

Commercial space leases are complicated. Work with a commercial real estate agent or a lawyer to help you negotiate the best terms.

A commercial real estate agent can help you

determine cost per square foot or cubic metre. They will know what permits you need and what inspectors need to be called. They are experts on where to find a serviced site, negotiating the various regulations of your city (or town, county or region), and determining your cost of build-out.

## I want to move to another state or province. Does it make sense to create a job for myself by buying a franchise?

Rather than "job," think of the life you want to lead. Draw a pie chart, dividing it into slices representing work, family, friends, leisure, spirituality and any other important segments of your life. Fill in what you want, and what you need, in each one.

Now, take a closer look at what you have written in the work slice.

The advantage of franchising is that it will help you get established in your new home market. Before you arrive, the brand is already known. The franchisor will also help with finding the right location All franchisors do a lot of handholding with their new franchisees, particularly pre-opening and in the first few weeks.

The one disadvantage you will have is that your current community – the people you know, work with and perhaps volunteer with – would naturally be your first customers. If you are the type who makes friends quickly, then you are likely to quickly build a new network of friends and customers in your new community.

If you are shy or slow to make friends, it will be harder, but that would be true anywhere, and may mean that franchising is not for you.

## How is being a franchisee different from being an independent business owner?

As an independent, you do all the work. As a franchisee, you have a franchisor that is focusing on building brand equity, product development, national advertising, and (usually) supplier relationships that provide for preferential pricing (group buying power). This frees you to concentrate on serving customers and the day-to-day operation of the business.

## What if there is a major change in my life and I can't run my business? Could I sell my franchise?

Usually yes, under conditions stated in your Franchise Agreement.

## What if I want to retire before the term of the franchise agreement is completed? Can I do that?

Exit strategies are usually covered in detail in the Franchise Agreement (if they aren't, you and your lawyer will want to write this in). It's smart to exit smiling. To make sure this will happen at some future date, you need to plan for it.

If you exit before your Franchise Agreement term has expired, some franchisors require that you find the next franchisee (they retain the right to accept or refuse your choice). Others reserve the right to 'buy back' the franchise, then may run it as a corporate store while they look for a suitable new franchisee. Either way, there are exit costs. Usually, franchisors also reserve the right to approve the price (for fair market value) when you are selling to the next franchisee in your location.

Generally, if you want to get out of your deal in the early years of the term, you will have relatively little equity in the business (assets plus goodwill) to sell to the next franchisee. It makes sense, going in, to have a personal Plan B (in the event of, for example, a health emergency) in mind. That Plan B could be a spouse or relative or employee who works in and knows the business is ready and willing to step into your role in your absence.

## What other reasons are there for franchisees leaving the business early?

There are plenty of reasons in addition to a health

issue. Among them:

- You get bored or want a new challenge.
- Your spouse is transferred to another city or part of the country or abroad.
- You cannot make a profit in this business.
- The desire to move up or to downsize.
- A poor choice; bad fit with the concept.
- Partner or shareholder disputes.
- Franchisor/franchisee disputes that cannot be resolved.
- Under-funded; cash flow problems.
- Personal problems, illness, divorce.
- Profit-taking (exiting the business is the only way to realize the increase in equity in the business created through the franchisee's efforts).
- A choice to return to the corporate world as an employee or to start your own business, become a consultant or change careers.
- The opportunity to become a Sub franchisor or manager.
- The choice to become a franchisee of a different banner.

## Can my children inherit my franchise?

In franchising you do not own the business, so, no, they cannot inherit ownership of the business. What you *do* own is the right to run your unit of the business and profit from it for the term of your Franchise Agreement.

In most Franchise Agreements, the term is not automatically assumable by your heirs, although if they have been active in the business, the franchisor will consider them as the next franchisee for that location, usually requiring them to meet the same qualifications as any other new franchisee.

In the early years of the term, your assets in the business may be relatively small, while in later years they could be much larger and therefore be an asset your heirs could sell back to the company, or to the next franchisee (under the conditions of your Franchise Agreement). As a franchisee, your assets in the business are goodwill, and perhaps current inventory, plus the value of leases or equipment owned by the business (such as service vehicles).

This is another area to discuss with your lawyer. If this is something you want, check to be sure the franchise is assignable (your equity can be inherited) and that it may be sold by you, or by your heirs.

You may also own your work premises, although (with the exception of home-based businesses) a franchise is usually operated in leased commercial property, with the lease held by the franchisor or the franchisee.

In the event that the business will be sold, its assets will need to be valuated. There are franchise consultants who are able to do this task or you may use the services of a professional small business valuator (get referrals from the franchisor, other franchisees and your accountant).

Generally, when a franchised business is sold, the franchisor will reserve the right to scrutinize the buyer as thoroughly as they do any prospective franchisee. They retain the right to veto the sale if they have doubts about the incoming franchisee as well as for other reasons. Ask your lawyer about what these are in your Franchise Agreement before you sign.

## If I want to or need to exit before the term is up, will the franchisor try to prevent this?

Franchisees exiting early happens all the time, says Roger Noble, founder of Choice Corporation, a franchise consulting company.

Most franchisors do not want to be directly involved in the sale or financing process, but they do welcome ambitious, energetic new franchisees. If that is no longer who you are, for whatever reason, best to part company. Harmonious franchise family relationships are maintained when the franchisee moves on with the franchisor's blessing, says Noble, and wise franchisors know this.

## What are some of the major trends in franchising I should be aware of?

Look around you. What do you see as major cultural trends?

Listen to what people are talking about in coffee shops, at parties or meetings.

Read newspapers, magazines, and current bestsellers. Read business stories and follow business leaders online.

Watch TV news programs and documentaries.

The themes and trends shaping our culture are reflected everywhere around us, affecting every aspect of business, including franchising.

Some of these trends are:

1. **In developed nations, an aging population**. Despite all the appeals (movies, advertising) to youth, people in their 20s and Millennials, the fact is that a significant amount of buying power is held by people over age 45.

2. **Smaller families**. Two children, or an only child has become the norm, while many couples opt for no children.

3. **Dual income earning families.** Few families are able to (or opt to) live on one income. One of the results is the popularity of convenience and timesaving products and services.

4. **Health awareness**. Consumers expect to live longer, healthier lives. They expect to remain healthy until late in life. They expect to (as three out of four elderly people do) live out their lives in their own homes, perhaps with care assistance, rather than in a care institution.

5. **Job security** has vanished in almost every type of work. Workers now expect to have to change jobs more often than their parents or grandparents did. There is both more choice in types of jobs open to most people, and more job mobility.

6. **The Gig Economy**. Making a living by combining two or three part-time jobs, renting out part of your home to tourists (Airbnb), being a part-time driver (Uber) or starting a small home business on the side are some of the ways workers are supplementing their incomes.

7. **Use of Internet and Social Media**. Consumers have new ways to receive information, communicate about products and services and many now expect to be able to shop online.

8. **The post-WWII generation,** the boomers, have redefined every life stage as they attained it. Now, they are changing our perceptions of "retirement" and "ageing."

All of these trends are reflected in franchise opportunities, some of which did not exist even 10 years ago. The rise of home-based elder-care (families too busy to do routine tasks for elderly relatives), the surprising explosion in the tutoring industry (driven by parents' perception that their children will face tough competition to get accepted at the top universities or to win entry-level jobs in the most sought-after professions), and health foods including sports supplements retailers and nutritional juice bars (for the health-conscious) are a few of these opportunities. Others are in all-natural or organic products such as make-up and grooming products.

If you want to know which franchisors will be on the hot franchise lists a year from now, or two, or three, just read the news and spot the trends. Then think, how are consumer demands changing? What products and services will people want and be willing to pay for? And who will provide them?

As to what current 'stars' may fade, my advice is steer a wide berth around franchises that are:

In a market that is crowded with competitors (a saturated market),

With low entry barriers, meaning competition may only increase,

Appealing to too narrow a demographic group,

Or have a very narrow season when their goods or services are sought by customers,

Or have too heavily relied upon only one or a few products,

Or offer a narrow product range that may prove to be a fad, or

Offer products or services with no distinctive competitive advantage, or one that customers do not want and are not willing to pay for.

## I want to play it safe. What are the real perennials among franchise systems? Ones that seem poised to be profitable for a long time to come?

These are:

- Anything to do with cars including rental, repair or parts replacement.
- Drug stores. But be aware that for some banners only pharmacists qualify as franchisees.
- Real estate. Usually franchisees must be qualified brokers.
- Services. The fastest growing sector of the economy, also accounts for the hottest franchise opportunities, a trend expected to continue through-out the 21st century. Especially hardy are education and health care.

## How do I get to meet the CEO or President or Founder of the franchise system I am interested in? And, when I do meet him or her, what questions should I ask?

In smaller systems, you will have this opportunity. But if, for example, you want to open one of the majors, you will meet a few VPs but it is unlikely you will meet the founder or the current CEO.

If (or when) you do meet the CEO, they will assume:

- You have read all of the materials sent to you by the franchise manager.
- You have been a customer at several of their locations.

- You have talked to their franchisees.
- You have talked to their customers.
- And that you've done your due diligence. You know their products and their brand, who they appeal to and why.

Here are some questions you could ask that will not only engage their attention, but also reveal the character of the company:

- What do you see as the top trend in this industry and why?
- What charities are you involved in, and why? What level of franchisee involvement is there with these charities?
- Where will this company be in two years? In five?

In the (extremely) unlikely event that you find yourself seated next to the CEO, say on a flight to somewhere, here are a few good conversation openers:

- What, in your opinion, is the second best franchise opportunity out there, and why?
- Who were your mentors, and what did you learn from them?
- Who do you admire most in this industry, and why?

## What is a guarantor? Do I need one?

If the franchisor or your lender has any reason to

doubt your ability to meet your financial obligations, one or the other may require a person who could meet those obligations to co-sign. That person is your guarantor.

There are some good reasons not to have your spouse as your guarantor, among them not exposing him or her to your financial risk, especially if your spouse is not going to be involved in the business. Failure could mean loss of personal assets for both you and your guarantor, and that can include a family home and retirement savings.

Speak to your accountant and your franchise lawyer and you may also want to consult a tax lawyer before you sign with a guarantor.

## What happens during training? What does it usually include?

Training is one of the benefits you receive in exchange for the Franchise Fee, and is usually two or three weeks, though it may be as brief as a few days or as long as a few months. It may be presented at head office, at a regional training centre, or in a corporate store.

It is usually designed to be intense.

Usually training is offered in two segments: classroom and in a working store.

The classroom section is a nuts and bolts approach to both business basics and the specifics of running this business, which will include how to open, how to close, and how to do the regular tasks of that particular business, such as clean the latte machine or re-glaze a bathtub or hire a homecare provider. You will also be walked through the Operating System Manual, with every step explained in full, and have the opportunity to have all your questions answered.

The second half of the training is usually in a working store or outlet, doing everything from serving customers to sweeping the floors. Think of this an immersion course in your new business with long days, hard work, but meant to get you up to speed fast while building your confidence: yes, you can do this!

## What is a business plan? Do I need one?

A business plan is a summary of what you plan to accomplish in business and how you will marshal resources to achieve your goals. The business plan is the road map, noting all the routes and any possible hazards along the way. Success is the destination.

By putting your plan in writing, you, your advisors and your lenders can clearly assess the SWOT of this business as you plan to organize and operate it. SWOT analysis is a business model – the Strengths, Weaknesses, Opportunities and Threats to success. It can help you to actually do a SWOT analysis for the business and a second one for *you* as a franchisee in this business, putting points under each of the four headings in bullet form.

Many franchisors and most lenders have a business plan template. You fill in the information. There are good reasons why you should do this yourself, not hire someone to do it for you:

- It requires that you think about, plan, budget and forecast results. It causes you to set measurable goals and attach timelines to these goals.

- The business plan will become the basis for your bookkeeping systems.

- It defines what will be the break-even point in profitability, anticipated cash flow and anticipated return on investment (ROI).

- It helps investors, potential partners, or lenders assess the merit of your plan.

- It helps you and your expert support team anticipate problems (such as being under-capitalized).

- It is an analysis of the skills assets (in addition to your own) that will be needed, for example identifying the number of employees needed, when they will be needed and the salaries they will be paid.

- It puts numbers to your plans. It is a business truism that you cannot manage what you cannot measure.

- It demonstrates your professionalism.

- It links your personal goals with your business goals.

- It provides the initial strategy for your business and sets milestone accomplishments, with timelines. In future, you will look at your quarterly results and compare them to the business plan to see if you are on track.

- It causes you to do some honest self-assessment of your personal skills, strengths and weaknesses.
- It serves as the foundation for all future business planning and goal-setting.
- A carefully-considered business plan helps reduce risk by anticipating needs and developing strategies for any potential problems.

It may reveal that there is not enough potential profit in the business, too much competition in your market, too few potential customers or that this business will require more capital than you have, or a larger debt load than you had anticipated, or will not deliver the lifestyle you want. If so, you can change your plans before you have had the expense and pain of a business failure.

Here is what a business plan usually contains:

**1.** *A summary*:

One page or less about the business.

Defines what the business is, why it will succeed, how profitable it will be.

**2.** *An introduction*:

Name and address.

Description of the market area.

Securities offered to investors.

Business loans sought and for what amounts, including operating line of credit.

**3.** *The Business Concept*:

A full description of the industry (markets, customers, competitors).

How this industry is affected by consumer and economic trends.

Description of the products, services, business location and size, staff and equipment needed.

Goals (gross sales, profit margins, ROI) for first three years.

A marketing plan with the sales strategy, including how you will price, promote, and build the number of loyal customers.

Sales forecast, including sales assumptions and how you made these assumptions.

Monthly forecast for first year in business.

Production or suppliers (sources, volume discounts).

Cost of equipment, facilities, list of contracts and agreements.

Professional consultants, key management, brief job descriptions.

Risk assessment and the 'what if' contingency plans.

**4.** *The Financial Plan*:

Financial statements (if you are buying from a franchisee).

Opening balance sheet (for new store).

Projected income statements.

Cash flow forecast.

Loans being applied for and details of those loans.

**5.** *References*:

Your lenders, lawyer, accountant.

**6.** *Additional information and documentation:*

Lenders may require the following:

- Personal net worth statement.
- Personal cost-of-living budget.
- Projected financial needs for the first three months.
- Letters of intent.
- List of inventory.
- List of fixed assets.
- Product price lists.
- Description of insurance coverage.
- Any accounts receivable or payable (if purchased business).

## A friend tells me I need to incorporate. Is this true?

Your three options for organizing the business are sole proprietorship, partnership and incorporating. Each has advantages and disadvantages.

***Sole proprietorship*** is the simplest, easiest and fastest way to get started. In this format, you run the business in your own name, or through a registered trade name. The business income and your income are considered to be the same for tax purposes. The disadvantage is that you may pay higher taxes and you will be personally liable for the business and legal obligations of the business.

**Partnership** is two people, or a group serving as co-owners of the business. Partners are not required to own equal shares in the business.

The advantage is that you share the work and the liability, but that's also the downside because you can't fire a partner.

There may also some tax advantages, particularly in the early days of a business. However, some government loans, subsidies or guarantee programs are only available to corporations.

Partnership is a more complicated, more expensive option than sole proprietorship, but less so than incorporating.

**Corporation (or a Limited Company).** In law, an incorporated company has the same legal rights and responsibilities as a citizen. The advantage to incorporating a business is that it is the business that carries liability, not the owners even when all of the income from that business goes to the owners.

Therefore, the higher the potential risk, either financial or legal, the greater the need to incorporate.

Corporations imply higher prestige, more stability and greater resources. The disadvantages are this is a more expensive and complex business legal structure.

There are more required licenses, reports and other requirements. Determining taxes and tax reporting is more complex.

Franchisors may also raise concerns when you incorporate because they will be getting the signal that you wish to escape personal liability in case of business failure.

The business structure that will work best is something else to add to your list of topics to discuss with both your lawyer and your accountant.

## What is a master franchisor?

When a franchisor wants to expand into a major region of the country, such as, for example, the Northwest, they may seek a master franchisor (sometimes also known as master franchisee) that has the responsibility to find new franchisees for that area and train them. The master franchisor functions as the franchisor in that area, but the ongoing support is usually provided to franchisees by both the master franchisor and the franchisor (head office).

The master franchisor may also be a franchisee of his or her own stores or units and, in addition, earns a percentage of the royalty payments paid by each franchisee in his or her area. However, the franchise agreement is directly between each franchisee and the franchisor.

A variation is Sub-Franchising. A sub-franchisor recruits new franchisees, develops the area, provides training and does the site selection. In Sub-franchising, franchisees deal entirely with the Sub-franchisor.

Offshore franchisors (successful abroad but unknown here) also may use this method to grow their banner by appointing an American or Canadian Sub-franchisor, which grants the right to act as franchisor for the entire country. The Sub may, in turn, grant master franchisors for regions of the country.

Another term you may hear is *Area Development*. An Area Developer is the same as a Sub-franchisor with the exceptions that the area developer can either open its own corporate units or recruit franchisees, as long as the Area Developer opens a stated number of units within a stated period of time or before a deadline. The area developer may be paid part of the franchise fee and earn a percentage of the royalties of all units in his or her territory.

## Distributorship, licensing, business opportunity, franchise – are these all words for more or less the same thing?

In a *Distributorship*, the business is independently owned and the owners have agreed to sell, exclusively, the products of one (or related) manufacturers who supply product at wholesale prices.

Unlike a franchisee, a distributor does not pay royalties, and the manufacturers of the product do not dictate the method of operating the business, though they may provide staff training and advertising/marketing assistance.

While distributorships are usually business-to-business, **dealerships** are like distributorships, except they sell directly to consumers.

**Licensing** is granting the rights to use patents, trademarks or other business knowledge without prescribing how the license-holder will run his or her business, usually for a given period of time.

**Franchising** is also known as business-format franchising. It involves both the licensing of a product or service and provision of the method of how to run the business (OS) for a given period of time (the agreement term).

Be aware that some "opportunities" such as schemes to 'Own your own cash machine' (in which you purchase an automated teller machine and then make your own arrangement about where to place it) and vending machine routes may represent themselves as "franchise opportunities," but are, in fact either a simple purchase, in the case of the ATM, or distributorships.

## What is the debunking session?

The point (usually just before signing a franchise agreement) at which you find yourself speaking to a senior manager of the franchisor. He or she will ask the sales person to leave the room for a few minutes.

They want to ask if you have received an accurate representation of this opportunity and its potential earning power. In small systems, this may be the founder or president who is doing the asking, but in most it is more likely to be a VP.

What they are looking for is an assurance that you don't have stars in your eyes. Yes, they want you to be in love with the concept, but they also want to know you are an optimistic realist and are practical and sensible enough to be entering this relationship fully informed.

Their fear is that if it all turns sour, you couldn't legitimately claim, at some future date, that the opportunity was misrepresented and earnings potential overstated by the sales person.

## Is there a downside to franchising?

Contrary to the claims of some Franchise Brokers, there is a downside to everything, even franchising.

In franchising, your major insurance against making a big mistake is in doing thorough, careful, thoughtful due diligence, including answering those tough and personal questions about who you really are and what you want.

Skipping your homework now will (barring the kind of crazy luck that few people have except in TV sitcoms) lead to a poor choice or a mistaken view of what is involved.

Pitfalls can be:

**1. Straying from the franchisor's system**.
Difficulties arise when a franchisee may have a different, possibly better, way of doing something, but that is not the way the OS dictates it be done.

To be a success in franchising you must be able to do it their way. The great strength of franchising is consistency, and that means compliance. If this will be too restrictive for you, it is much better to discover this before you invest in a franchise and the franchisor invests time and managerial resources in you.

**2. Loss of independence**. Some franchisees are surprised to learn the amount of control franchisors have. To free spirits, becoming a franchisee may be something like joining the military and never getting out of boot camp. Unless you can accept a certain amount of structure and routine (the free spirits might call it "regimentation"), franchising may not be for you.

**3. Not taking the time to fully understand your Franchise Agreement.** The best advice you will get is to hire competent experts, including a franchise lawyer who can fully explain every section of these complex contracts.

You need to understand the Franchisee/Franchisor relationship, which is a partnership that is in some ways like a marriage. Both sides give up some freedoms, take on new responsibilities, make a long-term commitment and must work well together to achieve success.

**4. Franchisor failure**. It pays to know as much as

you can about a franchisor before you join their flock. Franchisors have failed in the past. When they hit challenging times, they failed to deliver the benefits or the support they promised, due to their own staff problems or cash flow shortfall. Perhaps they oversold the opportunity. If it was not accurately described, it is referred to as *misrepresentation*. This may have been a mistake on the part of the franchisor. They simply did not understand your market's demographics, for example.

Or, worst case, it may be that the figures they supplied are total fabrications. This is why doing your due diligence is critical. In franchising, as in making any investment, it is buyer beware. If you don't trust them, don't sign!

## Once my new business opens, what sort of support can I expect from head office?

Franchisors do everything to free you to concentrate on the day-to-day running of your unit. From the franchisor you can expect:

- Visits – Someone from head office (or their area representatives) will come to both offer their assistance and check up on you for OS compliance, usually two or three times a year.
- On-going marketing and marketing research.
- On-going product development.
- Business forecasting.

- Changes and improvements to the OS.

- Tech that may include Intranet (an internal net, perhaps with an information exchange or franchise chat area, newsletter, training for yourself or your staff and new product information) or group software (for inventory control, payroll, or other HR or accounting tasks).

- Supply chain –group buying power can be a significant competitive advantage.

**What if I have a problem with the franchisor and we can't agree? Say they want to bring in a new product that I don't think is going to fly with my customers?**

**Or what if customers keep telling me, "Maybe you can charge that much in the city, but here? Forget it. I can get it down the street for cheaper!" Can I lower my prices? Can I just not carry a product? What can I do?**

Part of the experience for customers (and this is key to why franchising is so successful) is that they recognize the brand. Before they even come into your store they know what kind of products you have, what the buying experience will be like and what they expect to pay.

When they are far from home, that brand can offer them comfort as well as service because it is familiar.

If you start changing the product, or the price, or anything else about the brand, not only are you confusing and disappointing customers, you are breaking the terms of your contract with the franchisor. The result can be serious, including losing business for you and for your colleagues who are the other franchisees in your system.

Inevitably, the franchisor finds out and then there will be warnings, and, if you ignore these, your contract could be cancelled and your investment in both money and time building the business will be gone.

Consider this story about one unit of a major international ice cream treats chain. When it came to the attention of head office that a franchisee in a small city was under-performing, they took a closer look and discovered that this franchisee was overcharging for products, while at the same time he had allowed the store to become run-down and hadn't replaced some of the equipment. He refused to correct the pricing and fix the broken tables and worn out equipment and ultimately his carelessness meant the franchisor exercised its right to cancel his franchise agreement.

Franchisors don't take this drastic step lightly. It's a lose-lose scenario. It also disappoints customers loyal to the brand. Recognizing this, the franchisor looked for an ambitious new franchisee.

With new signage, new furniture and equipment, fresh décor and the new franchisees this outlet is now a success.

"If you stay consistent, provide good food, good service, a clean store and hygienic employees, you can't miss," says a long-term franchisee of this banner.

## The franchise system I am interested in has a Franchisee Council. What is that?

A method of providing the franchisor with feedback from the front-line troops who deal directly with customers and for franchisees to communicate their concerns, problems, gripes and good ideas to the franchisor. Franchisee Councils are usually made up of franchisees selected by the franchisor.

Franchisors have found that Franchisee Councils not only improve two-way communication with franchisees, but can also be a conduit of ideas that benefit everyone in the system.

## Say I think of a terrific new product I know our customers would love, or come up with a better way to do something. Can I test it in my store?

No, because that is specifically prohibited in the Franchise Agreement and the Manual and doing so could be a contract-breaker.

There are better ways to suggest new products to

your franchisor. The primary one is to send the idea to your representative on the Franchisee Council, if your franchisor has a Franchisee Council (all the biggies and most of the rest do. If your system doesn't, suggest it). Or, you could send the suggestion to your Area Rep or Master franchisor or the person at head office you deal with.

Many franchisors, and particularly the smaller and newer systems, actively seek ideas from franchisees and all of them have changed products, or introduced new ones, in response to customer demand. Even in the big, well-established systems a bright franchisee idea can prove to be a winner for everyone in that system.

**Right now, I'm a nurse and I'm approaching burnout. I want to make a total change in my working life and franchising looks like a way to make this happen. But I've never done anything else, aside from student jobs. Maybe this isn't such a good idea?**

Desire tends to draw us to what we are meant to be doing in life, as opposed to what we 'should' be doing.

Think about the skills you have and your experiences, both in nursing and from other areas of your life, in other roles (perhaps as daughter, mother, wife, friend, volunteer or mentor). And think about the accomplishments in life that bring you the most pride and satisfaction.

Chances are, there is a direct link to what you dream of doing in your next career.

If you feel strongly that you are meant to be a franchisee, but you have no related experience to point to as proof of this, you may have a harder time than the 'average' franchisee applicant in convincing the franchisor of your potential.

If you have thought carefully about what you have done so far in life in addition to nursing, you will be able to point out to the franchisor the value of your transferable skills and life experiences. For example, your list might include working with difficult people, working with little supervision, perseverance, ability to oversee the work of staff and problem-solving.

One way to convince a franchisor that you are a serious contender, and an excellent way to get a true insider's view of the business, is to work as a staff member for another franchisee in the system for a while. [Recognizing the value of this strategy, some franchisors actually require franchisees to do this.]

If you like what you see, and have impressed the franchisor with your can-do spirit, you have a great shot at being one of their star franchisees in future.

 This worked for one franchisee that had spent four years as manager of a downtown nutrition store, before he became the franchisee of his city's north end store. "After working for them, I know they are straight-up, honest and they do what they say they'll do," he says. "That's the value of a recognized name."

One woman started behind the counter at a large burger chain part-time when she was still in high school. Today, she is the franchisee of ten units, nine of them in downtown Toronto and one in a near-by suburb. "You'd be surprised how many successful franchisees in our system got started the same way," she says. "For most of us, it was our first job and for some, like me, it's the only place we've ever wanted to work. I can't think of a better way to learn about a business than by working directly with its customers!"

## What is the franchise life really like? What is the typical workweek for a franchisee?

To gain a good insight, if you can't work in another franchisee's unit, ask if you can 'shadow' a franchisee in the system you are seriously considering for several hours, and preferably for a 'typical' day.

Then ask yourself: "Can I see myself doing this? Would I enjoy it?"

The typical workweek is all or almost all of the usual working hours in that business (though you may have staff to open or close or take most of the weekend shifts or the night shifts), plus, generally, 10 to 15 hours a week longer than the number of hours worked by your top employee for administration/paperwork.

Yes, there is flexibility in work hours, though hours of operation may be dictated either by the franchisor or, if you have a mall location, set down in your lease agreement.

## It seems that most franchises are fast food. Why is this? Are fast food outlets the most successful?

About half of all franchised businesses' annual revenues are earned by fast food banners, including the QSR and fast casual burger, coffee-and-donut, pizza, ice cream, steak and ribs, fish and chips and chicken take-out and restaurant franchisors.

Due to massive marketing budgets, these fast fooders have done a remarkably successful job of getting the attention of consumers (and capturing our dollars) so, understandably, most people just assume that the definition of franchise is "fast food."

Not so. Dip into any franchising directory (see Resources) and you will find that franchised businesses cover a wide range of products and services.

QSR tends to be very high volume, but it also has higher entry costs and generally higher operating costs than other types of franchises.

## I already have a successful independent business, but think it could work as a franchise and I am seriously considering becoming a franchisor with this business.

# How do I find out if it could work?

If you can answer yes to the following questions, you could be right:

- Have you been in business for at least three years?

- Is the system transferable? Has it been successful at more than one location?

- Can this system be taught to almost any adult of average intelligence who does not have a background in this type of business? Can this training be delivered in a relatively short amount of time?

- Do you have a unique advantage in the marketplace?

- Do you have a tremendous amount of drive and energy?

- Do you have the money it will take for legal fees, to test your system and establish your company as a franchisor?

- Do you have a strong desire to help others succeed?

Franchise consultants and franchise lawyers can help you explore the options in converting your successful business to a franchisor.

# Why would any business franchise itself?

Here is what franchising looks like, from the franchisor's point of view.

They need growth and choose to do this through expansion. This means more stores, more locations. To do this, they need capital. One way to raise the funds is to sell a significant part of the business to shareholders (then this company is said to be publicly traded. The shares are listed on a stock exchange).

These shareholders then control the company as its owners, but they are 'passive' owners because, while they are investors, they do not work in the company. The company is actually governed by a board of directors (whose mandate is to maximize shareholder value) and run by its managers.

Another method is to become a franchise. In this way the company also acquires investors who use their own money to grow the business. Another benefit, to franchisors, is that these investors are active in the business. They are not merely managers, and thus employees. As franchisees, they have a personal stake in the success, plus a time commitment (the term of the Franchise Agreement).

A successful business franchises itself to grow quickly by attracting talented, committed, passionate people and give these people the conditions to generate success for both themselves and the franchisor.

## But will I get rich?

Yes, it could happen if you choose wisely, hire good

experts to guide you and believe that fortune smiles on those who strive for success while treating others fairly and honestly, with respect.

I wish you all the best and sincerely hope for *your* success.

JE Johnson

# *RESOURCES*

## *National Franchise Associations*

There are national franchise associations in every developed country. They offer information online about their franchisor members and other useful tools for prospective franchisees including articles and franchise trade show locations and dates.

On each of these sites you will find a directory of members seeking franchisees and also most have other useful tools such as listings of franchise consultants and franchise lawyers (who are usually associate members of the franchise associations).

The umbrella organization is International Franchise Association at **www.franchise.org**

United States, see the IFA site, **www.franchise.org**

Canada, Canadian Franchise Association, **www.cfa.ca**

New Zealand, **www.franchise.org.nz**

Australia, **www.franchise.at**

Britain, **www.british-franchise.org.uk**

China, **www.ccfa.org.cn**

For other nations, see **www.franchise.org** for a link.

## *Franchise Trade Shows*

The largest show in North America is the International Franchise Expo, held each spring in Washington, D.C.

This show is sponsored by International Franchise Association (I.F.A.) as is the fall version, held in a western state annually, the West Coast Franchise Expo.

For dates and details, see **www.franchise.org**


## *Magazines*

While franchising news is rarely reported in newspapers, it gets good coverage in business magazines. There are also several magazines that focus entirely on franchising.

**Entrepreneur** magazine is a business monthly that puts out an issue dedicated to franchising every January, including ratings on over 1,000 franchise opportunities in the U.S. and Canada. See **www.entrepreneurmag.com**

**Franchise Times** focuses each issue on one franchise sector, such as retail or health & beauty and also ranks the top 200 franchisors by number of units and sales. See **www.franchisetimes.com**

 **Franchise World** contains news, trends, events and people in franchising in the U.S., eight issues per year. See **www.franchise.org**


## *Directories*

**Bond's Franchise Guide**, is an annual listing of franchise companies operating in the U.S. and Canada, with more than 1,000 franchisors listed by name, address and contact person. Available at bookstores including Amazon.

**The Franchise Handbook**, available at **www.franchise1.com** is a quarterly directory of current franchisors seeking franchisees in U.S. and internationally; it also includes articles, success stories and information about franchise trade shows.

**The Franchise Opportunities Guide**, available at **www.franchise.org** is published semi-annually by the IFA. It also lists American franchise lawyers and consultants.

## *Web Sites*

**www.yourownfranchise.com** is the site of franchise consultant Greg Bast. It offers information and a free service that matches potential franchisees by preferences to current opportunities.

**www.franchise-consultation.com** free help in finding franchise opportunities by your preferences and types of opportunity. For example, there is a page of franchisors with low entry-costs for new franchisees.

# *GLOSSARY*

**Advertising Fund** – Fee paid monthly by franchisees into a fund controlled by the franchisor. Usually a percentage of gross sales (although in some franchise systems it is a set monthly amount), paid into a general fund out of which the franchisor buys national (and sometimes regional or local) broadcast (radio, TV), print (magazine, newspaper) and electronic (online) advertising.

The advantage to franchisees is in getting professionally-created ads, usually of a quality, distribution and frequency beyond what a small independent business would be able to afford.

**Banner** -- another word for brand, such as Minuteman Press or A&W. May also be used to refer to a franchise or the franchisor. For example, Mail Boxes Etc. is a system (a franchise) under the MBE Communications banner (the owner of Mail Boxes Etc.).

**Brand** – the identity of a product as perceived by customers and prospective customers. Includes the combination of the name, the logo and features/benefits associated with the franchisor's name and its products.

**Business opportunity** -- any form of investment to

generate revenue with the potential for profit, including franchising.

**Business plan**—description of the business. Includes financial plan, goals, strategies, analysis of competitors' strengths and weaknesses and how you propose to reduce risk. Required by lenders. Many franchisors and most lenders offer a Business Plan template.

**Capital required**—The franchisor's estimate of the amount of money a franchisee will need access to in order to operate the franchisee's new business until it is profitable (and therefore able to pay the franchisee a wage and meet all financial obligations of the business).

Usually franchisors base the amount of capital required for new franchisees on the experience of successful franchisees in that system.

**Churn** – Re-selling of an unsuccessful location that, for a variety of reasons, has not succeeded and probably cannot succeed, rather than closing it. A practice of unethical franchisors.

**Circular, The**—Disclosure Document. Required by law in several U.S. states (known as the Registration States), the **Uniform Franchise Offering Circular** (UFOC) includes information about the franchisor's business experience, litigation history, any restrictions on the franchisee's conduct of business, location selection, training and any celebrity involvement (spokesperson, endorsements) with the franchise. There are some variations between American states in how "franchise" is defined. See **Federal Trade Commission**.

**Co-branding**—when two banners share a location, and sometimes staff, to their mutual benefit, for example a Subway outlet located in a convenience store.

There are many variations including two franchises under one roof, or a franchise and an independent business, a franchisee and a corporate store, etc.. For all, the basic strategy is to create a method of reducing fixed costs (overhead), reducing some variable costs, appealing to 'non-traditional' potential customers and thus improving profitability for both brands.

**Copyright**—Protection by law of intellectual property (also known as knowledge assets). Combined with trademarks, copyright is the basis of brand value.

Brand value is one of the three primary assets the franchisee receives (in exchange for the Franchise Fee and Royalties) from the franchisor. Original works in the following categories can be copyright protected: literary (written), artistic, musical, dramatic, photographic and building design.

In franchising, copyright can be used to protect such assets created for and distinctive to the banner as words and art in advertising, logo design, product packaging, employee uniforms and advertising jingles.

**Corporate stores** – franchise outlets owned and managed directly by the franchisor. May be used for test marketing of new products and as a training site for new franchisees.

**Dealership**—Business model in which outlets are owned by entrepreneurs, usually with an exclusive relationship with the supplier.

**Debt-to-equity**--a critical accounting ratio, it compares what you owe to the total value of assets in the business.

**Deposit agreement**—Payment of earnest money by prospective franchisees. Used by franchisors to separate a genuine franchisee prospect from a mere tire-kicker. May be affected by specific legislation in your state and may (or may not) be refundable if you change your mind. Always discuss with a franchise lawyer before signing a Deposit Agreement. Also, see **Disclosure**.

**Disclosure**—information provided by franchisors to prospective franchisees about the company's financial health and performance, intended to help franchisees make informed decisions about investment. The specific information that must be delivered, and when, is regulated in most developed countries. The trend is to increased legislation to protect franchisees.

**Distributorship**—Business contact between a supplier and a product sales agent who may be a sales agency, wholesaler or retailer. Examples are truck, car and farm equipment dealerships, gas stations and regional beer or soda pop bottlers.

The difference between a distributorship and a franchise is that the distributorship is a method of selling product via independent owners, while the franchisee sells or distributes a specific product or service using the franchisor's trademark and operating system (OS) for a stated period of time (the term of the Franchise Agreement).

**Due diligence**—Business term meaning investigation of financials, usually as a condition of sale of a major asset. In franchising, due diligence refers to the careful investigation of a given franchisor's performance by a prospective franchisee before making a fully-informed investment decision. This investigation includes financials, products, support for franchisees and a consideration of the experiences related by current and former franchisees.

**Early entrant advantage**—business term referring to

benefits to individuals or businesses able to predict a major trend or demand in the marketplace and meet that demand the way a surfer meets a wave.

Pete Harman became the first KFC franchisee simply, he says, "because it is a good product," and so he not only helped define the franchise, but became wealthy in the process. Another early entrant with KFC was Dave Thomas. This self-described "fast food warrior" sold his restaurants back to KFC and became a millionaire, then started another franchise, known internationally as Wendy's.

**Fast casual**—a major trend in QSR, up-grading (usually existing) fast food outlets to dine-in restaurants catering largely to families and business people. Usually involves an expanded menu and larger seating area with relaxed theme and up-dated décor.

**Federal Trade Commission** (FTC) – American national regulatory body that is the watchdog for legislation stating the minimal amount of disclosure required in any of the 50 states, known as the **FTC Rule** (also known as Rule 436). In addition, several states have adopted their own rules and regulations that go beyond this minimum and apply to every franchisor doing business within their borders. Known as the Registration States, these include the states with the highest franchise and population density such as California, New York and Illinois. See **Circular**.

**Field consultant** – Employee of a franchisor who may provide franchisees with advice and guidance but whose main task is to assure the franchisor that the franchisee is following the OS.

**Franchise**—one unit of a franchisor's banner, operated by a franchisee. Also, the franchisee's right to operate his or her business using the OS and brand of the franchisor.

**Franchise agreement**—the contract between the franchisor and the franchisee, granting rights to the franchisee to operate the business using the franchisor's OS and brand.

**Franchise broker** – a salesperson or firm acting as an agent for one (or several) franchisor(s) to recruit new franchisees in exchange for a fee or commission paid by the franchisor.

**Franchise fee**--the initial or up-front fee paid by the franchlsee to the franchisor. Usually due at the time of signing the Franchise Agreement.

**Franchise lawyer** or **Franchise attorney** – lawyer who specializes in franchise law.

**Franchisee**—an individual who or company that

obtains the right to operate one or more units from the franchisor in return for payment of a Franchise Fee and Royalty payments.

**Franchisee council** – an advisory council of franchisees, representing the total group of franchisees, offering their insights on various issues to the franchisor.

All of the major franchisors and most of the rest (exceptions tend to be either very new systems that have not yet acquired a critical mass of franchisees or when it is a foreign franchisor relatively new to this country) either have or are developing franchisee advisory boards or councils. They are considered to be the most appropriate vehicle for franchisees to air concerns, grievances and ideas for product development or business growth.

**Franchisor** (or **Franchiser**) – the company that owns the rights to the brand and OS. May also refer to the founder of the company and its current senior managers.

**FTC** see **Federal Trade Commission**

**Goodwill**—a business term meaning all intangible assets built up in a company including its reputation and customer list.

**Guarantor**—When the franchisor has reason for concern that the franchisee has enough money to cover his or her obligations to the franchisor under the franchise agreement, the franchisor may seek a guarantee from a third party.

The Guarantor assures that the obligation will be met. When a potential franchisee chooses to incorporate, making the corporation the franchisee (and thus limiting personal liability) the Franchisor may ask for a guarantor.

**Initial investment**—Cost of starting the business, including the franchise fee, cost of the fixed assets (building, display equipment, vehicles, etc.), leasehold improvements (any improvements needed to leased location), inventory, franchise deposit (if there is one), franchise fee and working capital required for the start-up period.

**International Franchise Association (IFA)** – Umbrella association of national franchise associations.

**Intranet** —Intranet is an online, internal communications system. May be used to distribute news, broadcast messages, or for training for franchisees or their staff.

**Investment levels**—Level of resources needed to run

the business successfully. From lowest to highest: 1) home-based or vehicle-based service, 2) sales and distributorships or product-supply routes, 3) single unit retail, 4) multi-unit retail, 5) large-scale investments, such as hotels.

**Leverage**—business term referring to debt when compared to equity. Also refers to the use of borrowed capital to enhance opportunity for revenue generation.

May also refer to use of a non-financial asset, such as skills of the management team, to grow the business.

**Manual**—presents the OS. The basic how-to-succeed instruction manual given to new franchisees, outlining in step-by-step detail how to run the business. As part of the Franchise Agreement, franchisees are required to abide by procedures as given in the Manual.

Franchisors reserve the right to add to and update the Manual, which franchisees agree to abide by in advance (this is usually a condition stated in the Franchise Agreement).

**Master franchisor** or **Sub franchisor** or **Area Franchisor**—For a fee, a franchisor sells to (usually) a group of investors the right to use the brand (including its trademarks, trade secrets, logos, etc.) and to recruit, train and manage new franchisees in a given territory or region that may be a major section of the country or may mark the entry of this franchisor into another country. The Master or Sub does all of the usual functions of the franchisor within that region (or country).

**Mediation** – legal term. Method of dispute resolution that involves negotiation and strives for a win-win solution for both (or all) parties while seeking to avoid the damage to the relationship, time and expense of litigation.

**Multiple-unit franchising**—when a franchisee purchases the right to open and manage more than one unit, usually within a given time limit and within a defined territory such as all of a major city or an entire region of the country.

**Offering Circular**, or **Uniform Franchise Offering Circular** (UFOC)—Disclosure statement required of all franchisors doing business in the U.S., administered by the Federal Trade Commission. States that all prospective franchisees receive disclosure statements (the Offering Circular or The Circular) containing information about the franchise.

It must be delivered at the earliest of three times: the first face-to-face personal meeting with the franchisor; 10 business days before a franchisee makes any payment to the franchisor, or 10 days before signing the Franchise Agreement or any other contract imposing a binding legal obligation to the franchisee. See **Disclosure**.

**Operating System** or **OS** – the franchisor's success formula, this is the essence of what you get for the up-front fee you pay on signing the Franchise Agreement. As presented in training and in the Manual, the OS gives the how-to, when-to and where-to specifics (and sometimes also the why-to) of the business, usually step-by-step so that (almost) any adult could, with diligence, follow the formula and repeat the success of other franchisees in this system.

**Patriot Act**—In response to 9/11, the USA PATRIOT Act (for Uniting and Strengthening America by Providing Appropriate Tools Required to Intercept and Obstruct Terrorism) became federal law in the United States in 2001. The goal of this legislation is to follow the money trail used by international money launderers or financiers of terrorism. In practice, it gives the government additional powers to intervene in private business. In addition to broadening the definition of what is a crime and the laws of search and seizure, it imposes a number of financial compliance responsibilities including disclosure and reporting requirements.

The Patriot Act requires that businesses report to the Financial Crimes Enforcement Network (FinCENT) of the Treasury Department all transactions in which they receive more than $10,000 in currency. FinCENT has the power to subpoena U.S. businesses for any business records relating to customers, vendors or employees. As a result, franchisors are requiring franchisees to agree, in writing, that they will operate their new businesses in compliance with the Patriot

Act.

The Patriot Act applies to any business operated in the United States.

**Publicly traded**—a company owned by shareholders and traded freely on a stock exchange. The advantage to franchisees in investing in a publicly traded banner is increased regulation of the business (when compared to privately-held franchisors) results in increased information about the company, including financial information, is in the public domain and therefore available for scrutiny before signing the Franchise Agreement.

Examples of publicly traded companies that are franchisors are Berkshire Hathaway (owner of Dairy Queen) and Prime Restaurants (East Side Mario's). In practical terms, there is little difference for franchisees when their banner is publicly traded (versus private ownership).

**QSR**—stands for Quick Service Restaurant i.e. fast food.

**Re-franchising** or **Retro-franchising** – When a franchisor is selling a location that may have been a corporate store, or may have been run by a former franchisee, to a new franchisee with the expectation that the location will be successful. See **Churn**.

**Risk**—business term. Amount of exposure to the possibility of loss as a result of investment.

**ROI**—business term meaning return on investment.

**Royalty**—the way the franchisor earns its revenue. A percentage of gross sales or a set fee, paid by franchisees to the franchisor monthly.

**Service sector**—all businesses in which customers consume the primary product at the time that it is sold or delivered; the fastest-growing sector both in business and specifically in franchised businesses.

**Silent partnership** – a financing option offered by some franchisors to prospective franchisees who are fully-qualified but lack sufficient capital, which is provided by the partner or partners.

Silent partners are investors who are not active in the day-to-day operation of the business. Some franchisors help prospective franchisees find silent partners.

**Sub franchisor** – see Master Franchisor.

**System**—a franchise or franchisor. Also refers to the Operating System (see above).

**System standards** – standardized ways of conducting the business developed by the franchisor, usually presented in detail during initial training of new franchisees and in the Manual. Specifics of the success formula, which all franchisees agree to follow.

**Term**—is the time-span, in years, of a contract. The usual term of a Franchise Agreement is 20 years; through some franchisors offer terms of five or 10 years. Term is usually renewable for a further 5, 10 or 20 years, with payment of a fee by franchisees.

**Termination**—how the agreement between the Franchisor and Franchisee will end. Defined in the Franchise Agreement.

**Trade dress**—all the elements that make up the total image of a retail or restaurant business. May include interior and exterior design, lighting, signage, staff uniforms, product packaging and anything related that communicates brand awareness. Can be protected by trademark legislation if trade dress elements are used to identify this specific business and are distinct to the goods or services offered.

**Trademark**—A symbol, name or group of words, such as a slogan, that represents a company or its products, protected by legislation.

**Trade secrets**—A company's proprietary information, confidential formula, 'secret' recipe, business format and plan, prospect lists, pricing strategy and marketing and distribution methods.

To be a trade secret, the information must have commercial value, must not be generally known (or in the public domain) and the owner of the information must protect its confidentiality. As hundreds, and perhaps thousands, of franchisees will have access to the franchisor's trade secrets, franchisors require their franchisees to keep the company's trade secrets confidential.

**Turnkey operation**—A franchise provided to the new franchisee fully stocked and ready to do business.

**UFOC**--see Offering Circular.

**Unit** – a single outlet. In retail, one store. In a service franchise, usually one territory.

**Unit franchising**—franchising of a single outlet.